WOMEN & DEVELOPMENT IN MALAYSIA

Jamilah Ariffin

Pelanduk
Publications

Published by
Pelanduk Publications (M) Sdn Bhd
24 Jalan 20/16A, 46300 Petaling Jaya
Selangor Darul Ehsan
Malaysia.

All Rights Reserved.
Copyright © 1992 Jamilah Ariffin
Cover Design © 1992 Pelanduk Publications (M) Sdn Bhd
No part of this book may be reproduced or
transmitted, in any form or by any means, electronic
or mechanical, including photocopying, recording or by
any information storage or retrieval system, without
prior permission from the Publisher.

Perpustakaan Negara Malaysia
Cataloguing-In-Publication Data
Jamilah Ariffin
Women and Development in Malaysia/Jamilah Ariffin.
ISBN 967 978 410 X
ISBN 967 978 409 6 (pbk)
1. Women in development—Malaysia.
2. Women—Malaysia—Economic conditions.
3. Women—Malaysia—Social conditions.
4. Women—Malaysia.
I. Title
305.4209595

Printed by
Eagle Trading Sdn Bhd
81 Jalan SS25/32, 47301 Petaling Jaya
Selangor Darul Ehsan
Malaysia.

*This book
is dedicated to
my late mother, Zabedah,
for sensitizing me to the position
of underprivileged women of her generation,
and to
my two sisters, Puteh Mahiran and Rohana,
for representing the questioning women
of our generation.*

*And to
our young daughters,
Nurin, Thaera and Juwita,
may they strive for the betterment of
Women and Humanity in the future.*

JAMILAH ARIFFIN

THE AUTHOR

JAMILAH ARIFFIN is an associate professor in Rural Development at the Faculty of Economics and Administration, University of Malaya, in Kuala Lumpur, Malaysia. After completing her early education in Tapah, Perak, she went on to Victoria Institution, Kuala Lumpur, and later, proceeded to do further studies in Australia where she studied Sociology of Development at B.A. Hons., Master of Arts and Ph.D. levels. Dr. Jamilah has spent 18 years lecturing at three local universities. Her main research area is in Industrialization and Social Change with a special emphasis on Women Workers and Migration. She is currently the coordinator of the Population Studies Unit at the University of Malaya and the Research Committee Chairman of the National Advisory Council for the Integration of Women in Development (NACIWID). Her past involvements include being a member of the Commonwealth Expert Group on "Women and Structural Adjustment", a research coordinator of Royal Professor Ungku Aziz's HAWA Project on Women Factory Workers, and the team leader and research coordinator of IKWAM's project on "Poor Women of Malaysia".

CONTENTS

PREFACE
INTRODUCTION

1. The Historical Development Of Malaysia
And The Changing Role Of Women   *1*

2. Women's Productive Role
And Labour Force Participation   *30*

3. Women's Participation In Education In Malaysia   *54*

4. Women In Medicine
And Other Health-Related Aspects   *73*

5. Women In Organized
Movements And Government Service   *106*

6. The Development Of The Law
And Its impact On The Position and Status Of Women   *124*

7. Underlying Issues For Further Consideration   *171*

BIBLIOGRAPHY *175*
INDEX *181*

PREFACE

Since the 1970s there has been a growing demand among the general public in Malaysia for literature on women in development but there is still a scarcity of relevant publications. Similarly, there is a multitude of statistical data collected by various government agencies which pertain to women in development but there has not been any concerted effort to synthesize and to present them in simple terms. Just as planning without facts is akin to groping in the dark, similarly a mass of data without proper synthesis and analysis is like a heap of bricks which does not make a house.

In taking stock of the situation as described above, I decided to attempt writing a book on "Women and Development in Malaysia". The idea started as early as 1987 and the compilation of relevant data began in earnest in 1988. To aid this venture, I initiated and jointly organized a colloquium entitled "Women in Development in Malaysia: Implications for Planning and Population Dynamics" for the Population Studies Unit at the University of Malaya in January 1989. Several colleagues were invited to present research papers on the subject and the data which I had obtained and processed from various government ministries and libraries were supplied to some of them for this purpose. I therefore acknowledge the valuable contribution of these writers towards the formation of this book, particularly those whose work have been cited in the chapters. I would also like to urge readers to refer to all the citations in the text for elaboration on each of the subject matter. Some of these papers from this colloquium will soon be published in a book entitled *Readings on Women and Development in Malaysia*.[1]

Subsequently, the ideas crystallized within the local context were expanded through my brief sojourn abroad in 1989 to the Centre of Cross-Cultural Research on Women at Oxford University and the Institute of Development Studies (IDS) in Sussex, England. Thanks are due to Dr Shirley Ardener and Dr Soraya Trimayn of Oxford University and Dr Naila Kabeer of IDS for their hospitality and assistance which enabled me to gain access to the libraries and relevant research materials.

When reading this book, readers are requested to take note of a number of qualifiers. Firstly, the style of writing is geared towards the general reader and as such, academic jargon and complicated theoretical concepts are kept at a minimum. However, this does not mean that academic theoretical frameworks and ideas do not inform the analyses; it only means that these are not spelled out in detail.

Secondly, the tendency to describe the nuances of each subject matter may seem unnecessary to the academic reader but this is purposely done so as to enable the general reader to make their own analyses and conclusions. The orientation of the book is therefore to inform as well as to educate. It can also be easily utilized by academic researchers as background material for more detailed studies on focused research topics. Thirdly, the statistical data cited in the text pertain to the years before 1991. Events which occurred after December 1990 are not included. In a situation of rapid advancement in women's incorporation into development planning and implementation in Malaysia, a book project which involves a gestation period from the point of preparing and actual publication and which deals with data on women in development has to share a similar fate of a "fast-breaking story" as pointed out by Alvin Toffler in his book, *Future Shock*.[2]

Fourthly, much of the ideas and information contained in this book have been aired by the writer at various brainstorming sessions organized by various women's organizations and elaborated in written submissions to the relevant government departments in formulating the National Policy on Women as well as in preparing for the Chapter on Women and Development which was subsequently printed in the Sixth Malaysia Plan (1990–1995). Readers may want to read the Chapter in the Sixth Malaysia Plan for more up-to-date information pertaining to some of the aspects cited in this book.

Special thanks and acknowledgements are extended to Pelanduk Publications for their continual assurance to publish this piece of work and to Ms Debbie Leon for her research assistance. A personal note of appreciation is also specially accorded to Ms Rohinee Serisena for her efficient typing of the manuscript.

NOTES

[1] All the papers presented at the Colloquium are already printed in "Proceedings of the Colloquium on Women and Development in Malaysia", compiled by Jamilah Ariffin and Siti Rohani Yahya, Population Studies Unit, University of Malaya, 1990.

[2] Alvin Toffler, *Future Shock*, Random House, New York, 1970, Introduction, p. 6.

INTRODUCTION

The crux of this book is that women of Malaysia have since unrecorded history played a significant role in almost all spheres of the economy and society. Yet, why is it that only recently, beginning in the 1970s, that there is a call to "integrate women in development"? Why is it that it was only in the 1980s that we hear of Women as an important component of Human Capital and must necessarily be included in national development plans? To understand the series of events and forces leading to this growing realization about women's economic potentials and contribution, we must first of all have a good grounding on the history of Development in this country and how women were affected by this development process. It is also equally important that we assess the progress made by women in mainstream development of the nation's economy, polity and society as well as the factors facilitating this participation. While on this note, we must also be fully aware that although local gender ideologies shape the manner in which women are incorporated into the development process, the role of extraneous intervening variables such as the influence of market forces and political events outside the national economy also affect the rate and pattern of women's entry into mainstream development activities. Similarly, globalization trends and the generative nature of international contacts, ideas and ideologies also affect the manner in which the Malaysian Government perceives its womenfolk, how women and women's organizations perceive themselves and their roles, and how they demand for their integration into mainstream development. We should also realize that although development brings about new opportunities for women, it also recreates new inequalities not only *between* women and men but also *among* women in terms of class and ideological alignments. The above are the main thrusts of this book and it seeks to address the following issues discussed below.

In what sectors has the economic development process benefited women and in what aspects has it generated unfavourable effects on women's position and status? What are the main factors facilitating women's entry into mainstream activities in the organizational structure of the state bureaucracy and political life of the nation? What are the ideological orientations of the women's movement? What are the laws affecting women status? Should the health and medical system be improved to incorporate women's new needs and wants?

Chapter One begins with a historical analysis of the development of the Malaysian nation and explains the position of women at various points of this transitionary process moving from a milieu of feudalistic kingdoms to that of a colonized country and eventually towards the status of a modern nation state. It also traces the path of women's participation in the economic and political life of the nation and the vital role played by the formal education system in facilitating women's entry into mainstream development. It highlights the impetus generated by the United Nations Decade for women leading to greater acknowledgement of women's role by development planning agencies.

Chapter Two looks at the impact of the economic development process on women in terms of their economic participation and assesses its effects on women's position and status. Without attempting to go into the intricacies of the debate centring the various theories dealing with the effects of economic development on women or to ascertain the position of Malaysian women in terms of these theoretical frameworks,[1] the aim of this chapter is to provide a simplified explanation of how the encroachment of the capitalist economic system upon the indigenous economy in the Malay Peninsula has in fact caused an undervaluation of women's actual economic contribution. Although much of women's work continued to be indispensable and valuable to the economic life of the society it became invisible in national statistics on the labour force and economic activities. Another effect of the capitalistic system is the trend towards displacing women from mainstream agricultural activities and making them incapsulated within the trappings of "a farmer's wife", eventually causing a further gap in their economic progress *vis-à-vis* men and other women who meanwhile were steadily being absorbed in the structural process towards an industrialized and tertiary-based economy. However, the bulk of these other women (who were integrated into the modern economy, particularly in the industrial and services sector) were streamed mainly into a gender-based segmented labour market and into low-paying jobs with limited promotion opportunities, thus further strengthening gender inequalities.

As pointed out earlier, formal education is one of the most important facilitator for Malaysian women's confident participation in mainstream development. It was in fact the initial passport for women's departure from the confines of the domestic domain and their progressive inroads into salaried positions in the expanding bureaucracy as well as into top political positions. Chapter Three provides a historical analysis of women's growing access to formal schooling within the context of different developmental phases of the Malaysian education system. It also assesses the existing gap between men and women both in terms of literacy and level of educational attainment as well as in the pursuit of professional qualifications. Since most discourse on education tends to overlook the important role of non-formal education system in providing skills to those who cannot participate in, or are drop-outs from the formal education system, this chapter also discusses the types and range of non-formal education programmes available to Malaysian women within the urban and rural areas.

The underlying theme of Chapter Four is that the orientation of health and medical care system of a country all to often reflects the States' ideological perception of women's expected role and functions as well as the extent of gender equality which is permissible. It begins by highlighting the essential importance of health care and medical services for women because of their biological system and their reproductive role as prescribed by societal norms. It explains the general health status of the female population in Malaysia as indicated by statistics on mortality trends, maternal mortality and infant mortality rates. It then looks into the changing marital and fertility patterns which commensurate with the country's progress towards a more advanced economy. It also assesses the situation of health facilities and maternal care services. Although it acknowledges that there has been very significant progress made in the delivery of child and maternal health services especially by the government sector, what is of central concern in this chapter is the extent to which this can be further improved and that it should incorporate a more gender-sensitive approach in its policy formulation and implementation.

Chapter Five traces the path and changing orientation of the women's movement in Malaysia, women's involvement in the political arena and women's growing participation in the government service. It is shown in this chapter that the orientation of the women's movement has often been influenced by the changing trends in the women movements in the international arena although this is not to deny that much indigenization of ideas and approaches take place when tackling women's issues in the local scene at the appropriate time and place. These are in fact positive indicators of the growing maturity of the women's movement and the willingness to "keep up with the times". How the mass mobilization of women for political objectives began after the Second World War is explained and the steady inroads of women leaders into state and national-level politics is analysed. Taking the Government service as an example of the expanding bureaucracy, this chapter traces the participation pattern of women in various divisions of the organizational hierarchy and the categories of jobs where most women are concentrated in. However there are already positive indications that women are making significant inroads into higher positions.

Chapter Six looks at the development of the Law in Malaysia and its impact on women's position and status. Similar to other countries practising the "rule of Law", the Malaysian Law legitimizes the status quo as well as defines the boundaries for permissible conduct. Gender relations and its control over women's permissible boundaries are therefore reinforced by the Law. In attempting to treat all citizens, regardless of their sex, as equal, the Law makes no reference to gender. There are however several laws which favour men and in that manner discriminates against women particularly in matters relating to guardianship rights and citizenship for foreign spouses. Traditional values and norms which dictate that men are leaders and women are followers especially in a marriage are clearly reinforced by these laws. Laws which espouse to protect women workers are questioned in this chapter as to the extent they really protect women's interests, and hence the need for review.

Recent developments in the Law, especially the anti-rape laws, are also discussed.

Finally, Chapter Seven focuses on some of the main underlying issues of this book which require further consideration.

NOTES

[1] For example, Ester Boserup's theory on the effects of Economic Development on Women. See Ester Boserup's *Women's Role in Economic Development*, Allen and Unwin Ltd., 1970.

1

The Historical Development Of Malaysia And The Changing Role Of Women

Malaysia's history records a remarkable development. From a country once exporting merely primary products, Malaysia is now rapidly becoming one of the Newly Industrialized Countries (NICs) of the world. Malaysia also boasts a rich and colourful past, populated with Sultans and warriors, envoys and merchants, colonizers and nationalists, capitalists and indentured labourers. It is against this varied backdrop that we are going to view and understand the evolving role of Malaysian women.

As a nation develops, it is inevitable that the role of its women will also undergo changes. It is the aim of this chapter to trace the historical development of Malaysia and its impact on the role and status of women. The discussion will be based on women in three different historical eras, namely, the pre-colonial period, the colonial period and the post-colonial period. It will also look into the role of women in the various spheres of politics, economy and education within the context of Malaysian history.

THE PRE-COLONIAL PERIOD

Tanah Melayu, or Malaya—as Peninsular Malaysia was then known—was a part of the Malay Archipelago. The Malay Archipelago comprised of countries now known as the Philippines, Peninsular Malaysia, parts of Borneo and Indonesia and Singapore. Migration between these countries in the Malay Archipelago had started 11,000 years earlier and had continued either for purposes of trade or as people moved in search of greener pastures.

One such person was Parameswara, a Malay leader, who left Palembang, a kingdom in the island of Sumatra, and headed first for Temasik—now known as Singapore—and then arrived in the peninsula of Tanah Melayu where he later founded Malacca in 1400, becoming the first ruler of the Malacca Sultanate. Through skillful diplomacy, Parameswara made diplomatic advances towards powerful kingdoms like Siam (now known as Thailand) and China. Malacca soon became a tributary of Siam, sending gift tokens of 40 taels of gold yearly, in the form of *bunga mas,* or artificial flowers made of gold. Malacca also established diplomatic relations with China when in 1403, the Ming Emperor, sent eunuch Yin Ching as an envoy to Malacca. Soon, a good diplomatic relationship was established between the two countries and envoys were frequently exchanged between the two kingdoms. Malacca had by then flourished as the regional trade centre of South East Asia and was frequented by traders from China, India, Arabia and Europe. However, not many of these traders made Malacca their permanent home. Thus, the permanent inhabitants of Malacca then were the Malays and the aborigines, or *orang asli.*

The Malay community that existed then were divided into two distinct classes, that is, the ruling class and the commoner class. At the top of the ruling class was the *kerabat diraja* (royal family). This was followed by the court officials and *kaum bangsawan* (nobility), the territorial chiefs and the warriors. The commoner class that existed comprised of the *rakyat* (commoners) inclusive of peasants and traders, the *orang berhutang* (debt-bondage serfs) and the *hamba* (slaves).

Consequently, the roles of women then were defined by the classes to which they were born. The two major classes of women were mainly the aristocrats and the peasants. Both sets of women played different roles in the economy and political sector.

The aristocratic women consisted of consorts, wives and family members of the rulers and Ministers. They did not exercise any direct or appreciable political influence. However, indirectly some aristocratic women did foster better political connections with other kingdoms through marriages. Nevertheless, in a few states, especially in the event of the absence of male heirs, aristocratic women did participate directly in the political field. Patani, for example was once ruled by a queen, namely Raja Ijau. Kelantan too had a female ruler once. She was the famous Cik Siti Wan Kembang. As for the peasant women, they did not play any part in the political sector at all but participated directly in the peasant economy. Therefore, it can be said that men in that period dominated the political field as in any other patriarchal society.

Most aristocratic women did not take part in the economic sector and were mainly confined to social "reproduction", that is, the care and socialization of children and the maintenance of adult individuals who would fit into the social structure of society. However, there are some who owned land and engaged themselves in business activities such as tin-mining, trading and investing in debt-bondage slaves. The peasant women were the ones who took the more active part in economic activities outside the home despite their ordained roles as housewives and mothers. The reason for their active participation could be that they had the right to own land under customary laws or *adat* and the Islamic religion. For example, in any patriarchal Malay community which practised *Adat Temenggong*, women had an equal access to land as men, whereas in a matrilineal society which practised *Adat Perpateh*, women had the exclusive right to land. However, the coming of Islam altered this right and women were only entitled to half the man's share. Nonetheless, although patriarchy was the prevailing system, women did have access to productive assets, including land, and their position was not as subordinated as imagined because of the observance of the bilateral kinship system and flexible rules of conjugal residence.

Besides their vital role within the domestic domain, most peasant women were also actively involved in subsistence agriculture. Hence, they were involved not only in "reproduction" but in "production" as well. Food, like rice, was produced for self-consumption and to be traded in exchange for other necessities like salt and cloth. Both men and women laboured in the fields together to produce agricultural products but this does not mean that there was no allocation of tasks by gender. In padi planting, for example, women did most of the transplanting, weeding, winnowing and harvesting, whereas men did the ploughing and preparation of the fields, threshing and transporting of the rice. As for the fishing sector, the men would go out to sea while the women dried and processed the fish. Women mended the fishing nets too. The division of tasks was clear also in the handloom industry where, generally, the men would set up the loom and market the produce, whereas the women worked the loom. Women's position in relation to men was therefore often a complementary rather than a subordinate one.

In addition to the various sectors already mentioned, many peasant women were also actively involved in trading activities. This was true especially in the East Coast states where the majority of the traders in the marketplace were women. Older women would travel from place to place selling cloth or handicrafts. Women too were involved in tin-mining where together with the men, they would pan for tin using flat wooden trays called *dulang*.

All the above are examples of self-employed women. There were also those who worked in the palaces of the royalty. However, most of them were either debt-bondage servants or slaves.

Therefore, it can be said that women, especially peasant women, in the pre-colonial period, played an active part in the economic sector. The reason for this could be that besides having access to land, most of them had to learn to produce subsistence necessities. This was because with the existence of the *kerah* system—where commoners had to perform manual tasks for the ruling class once summoned—there would be times when the menfolk had to be away from home and the women would have to step in and take over their chores and responsibilities. During these spells, women became recognized economic producers. The process of production as well as reproduction was recognized as a unified activity. This view of women's role soon changed in the colonial period with the encroachment of the capitalist society and commercialized agriculture.

As for education, there was hardly any formal education in this period. Girls were generally informally educated. They were taught household skills and crafts by older women which were to help them fulfill their traditional gender roles in the domestic domain.

There is little in the historical records of this pre-colonial era on women of other races. The Chinese and Indians who came were mostly men and they did not make Malaya their permanent home. The first group of Chinese who set up permanent residence in Malacca was the entourage accompanying the Princess Hang Li Po, the daughter of the Emperor of China, who was sent to marry the Sultan of Malacca. They resided at Bukit China and their population was small. The Indian population in Tanah Melayu during this period was also small and predominantly male, for Indians, being a strong patriarchal society, believed that women should not leave their homes.

THE COLONIAL PERIOD

The following discussion will provide a brief history of Malaysia from the beginning of the colonial period until Malaysia's independence in 1957 and consider the role of women in politics, economy and education during this era.

The year 1511 marked the beginning of the colonial age, for in that year Malacca was conquered by the Portuguese. From that time onwards until its Independence in 1957, Malaya had been in the hands of a foreign power which ruled either directly or indirectly. In 1511, the Portuguese admiral, Alfonso de Albuquerque, conquered Malacca after a fierce struggle with the natives. The Portuguese then built themselves a powerful fortress in Malacca and ruled from within. Their aim, just like the Dutch after them, was to secure control over the important export trade of Indonesian spices, or *rempah*, and import activities dealing with Indian textiles. Thus, their rule in Malacca did not change the culture nor traditional livelihood of the local community. Later in 1641, Malacca was conquered by the Dutch. The Dutch too did not interfere with the existing culture and structure of society as their main interest was the monopoly of trade. The Dutch rule also witnessed the invasion of the Bugis from Acheh in the Johor kingdom which was part of the Malacca Sultanate. However, the intervention was only limited to the political field.

The real change to the lives of the local community and the role and status of women only began with British colonial rule.

On July 15, 1786, Sir Francis Light, leading a British force, occupied the island of Penang and made it the outpost for the British along the Straits of Malacca to function as a trade centre and a naval base. Penang was given to the British by the Sultan of Kedah who had hoped of gaining a foreign ally to protect his state from Siam. However, this hope was not realized. Later, in 1824, the Straits Settlements was formed after Singapore and Malacca had been obtained by the British. The settlements were ruled entirely by the British with no participation from the Malay community or the immigrants. In 1868, the Straits Settlements became a crown colony. Its guiding principle was non-intervention in the Malay states. Thus, the only relationship with the Malay states then was one of trade. In the early phase, the Straits ports would purchase what the states had to offer and in turn export manufactured goods and foodstuffs. However, the need to interfere in the Malay states soon arose in the 1870s. This was because the European countries were experiencing an industrial revolution, requiring an increase in the demand for tin and other raw materials. Thus, Chinese merchants from the Straits Settlements moved into the Malay states and began operating tin mines with labour imported form China. During this period, only the Malay ruling class in the Malay states participated in this new sector, whereas the peasant community was still confined to activities in subsistence agriculture.

Together with the labour migrants from China came groups of Chinese secret societies which caused riots and gang fights in the Malay states. This generated much concern among the Straits Settlements' traders who had invested in the Malay States. The Sultans' entreaties to the British authorities to quell the riots and maintain peace in the Malay States soon led to the signing of the Pangkor Treaty on January 20, 1874, between Andrew Clarke and Sultan Abdullah of Perak. The Pangkor Treaty marked the beginning of British intervention in the Malay States. Shortly after, Selangor, Negeri Sembilan and Pahang followed suit and in 1896 the Federated Malay States (FMS) was formed. In principle, each state was to be ruled by a Malay ruler. He, however, had to seek the advice of a British resident in all areas except religious and customary matters. Thus, in actual fact, the Resident was the one who ruled. Consequently, the lives of the Malay community slowly changed with the introduction of Western monopoly capitalism and modernization.

In 1909, the British extended its rule to four other states which were formerly "Siam Protectorates". These were Kedah, Perlis, Terengganu and Kelantan which together formed the Unfederated Malay States (UMS). In the case of the UMS, a British advisor was posted to each state but the Malay Ruler still held the ultimate political power. Thus, the British influence in the Unfederated Malay States was less than in the Federated Malay States and the local communities in these states did not experience as much change in their way of life. The state of Johor joined the UMS only in 1914.

Therefore, just before the Second World War, there were three forms of administration in Malaya, that is, the Straits Settlements, the Federated Malay States and the Unfederated Malay States.

The British colonial rule was interrupted by the Japanese invasion in the Second World War. The Japanese landed in Malaya on December 7, 1941 and by February 15, 1942, the British forces had surrendered in Singapore. The Japanese ruled Malaya for three years before they surrendered in August 1945. During this time, activities in the local economy came to a complete standstill. All exports were staggered as the estates and tin-mining industries had stopped functioning altogether. Imported goods, especially foodstuffs, were also scarce, thus many people suffered from starvation and malnutrition. The Japanese treated each major ethnic group differently. To the Malays, the Japanese gave the impression that they would restore the authority that was taken from them by the British. This encouraged many Malay Nationalist movements and saw the formation of societies such as the Kesatuan Melayu Muda (KMM). The Chinese were, however, treated badly by the Japanese. This was due to the Japanese' resentment towards the local Malayan Chinese' formal support for China during the Sino-Japan War. As a result, many Chinese joined the Malayan People's Anti-Japanese Army (MPAJA). The Indians were generally left alone but many were enlisted to build the "death railway" in Burma or join the Indian National Army to fight with the Japanese in Burma.

After the Japanese Occupation, Malaya was placed under the British Military Administration for seven months. Later, in April 1946, the concept of the Malayan Union was introduced but it met with a lot of opposition, especially from Malay political groups. Thus, the idea was abrogated, and in 1948 the Federation of Malaya was formed, whereby the Straits Settlements, Federated Malay States and Unfederated Malay States were united and administered by a centralized Government. Meanwhile, nationalism was spreading. Simultaneously, the threat of the communist groups was becoming more menacing. In 1948, an Emergency had to be declared over the whole of Malaya. It lasted for twelve long years.

After having experienced running the administration of the country on their own during the Japanese period, many locals were discontented at being governed by a colonial power. Political parties like the United Malays National Organization (UMNO), Malayan Chinese Association (MCA), Malayan Indian Congress (MIC) and others were formed. These parties lobbied for independence and in 1955 the first Federal Legislative Elections were held.

Finally, in August 31, 1957, Independence was declared and Tunku Abdul Rahman became the first Prime Minister.

Women And Politics During Colonial Rule

Since pre-colonial times, the political field had always been monopolized by men, and women had no part at all in it. Traditional society had always maintained that a woman's place is at home. Thus, despite her contribution to the economic sphere she was not to participate in the public domain.

However, with the introduction of formal education by the British in the 1930s, many women, especially those from the educated elite group, began to play a role in the public domain. They soon began to form voluntary associations. However, these associations had no political aims. Their objectives were simply to upgrade the lives of women. Thus, activities that were connected with the role of women as mother and wife, such as cooking, needlework and religious classes, were arranged. The first Malay women's organization formed was the Malay Women Teachers Union. It was founded by Hajah Zain Suleiman in 1929, with the aim of improving the knowledge of its members. Another important association was the Persatuan Kaum Ibu. This was set up in support of the political party formed by men from the Malay educated group as the sense of nationalism began to grow.

During the Second World War, most of the women's association ceased to function. However, new women's associations were established by the Japanese to foster communal organization and women were also recruited into the labour services corps. During this period many women were given the opportunity to participate in public lectures and rallies. This experience proved useful to women in the years to come. Nevertheless, it must be remembered that the women who were involved in such associations were mainly from the minority Malay elite educated group.

The Second World War brought about a lot of changes for women. During the war many women had to learn to fend for themselves and be self-sufficient. Thus, many traditions which had once inhibited women from participating in public life were now questioned. Soon, many women, especially Malay women, who were once bound by traditions became actively involved in politics which was once a field monopolized by men. Nevertheless, the immigrant women, like the Chinese, Indians and Eurasians were still involved mainly in non-political associations with the exception of those women who joined the Malayan Communist Party (MCP).

On March 1, 1946, the first Pan-Malayan Malay Congress was held and the Persatuan Kaum Ibu attended this congress. It was represented by Zaharah Tamin, Kamsiah Ibrahim and Siti Noraini Jenin. This reflects the gradual evolution of Persatuan Kaum Ibu from a non-political association into a political entity. The outcome of the congress was the formation of UMNO led by Dato Onn Jaafar. When the Malayan Union was first introduced, it was met with opposition. There were many political demonstrations and public rallies and many women participated in them. For example, Angkatan Wanita Sedar (AWAS) which was the left wing of the Malay Nationalist Party led many protests. There was an occasion when the Raja Perempuan Kelsom Laten, consort of the Sultan of Perak, personally led a procession as a sign of protest against the Malayan Union, brandishing banners with slogans like "Save the Malay Rulers". In 1949, the Persatuan Kaum Ibu was officially declared as the women section of UMNO and no longer a mere appendage of UMNO. Persatuan Kaum Ibu was now actively involved in recruiting new members, fund-raising projects and helping with elections as campaigners and voters. However, there were protests by some religious groups, like the Council of Ulamas, against women participating in politics. This was overcome by support from Tunku Abdul Rahman who became the next leader of UMNO, after Dato Onn. In 1955, Halimahton Abdul Majid became the first woman to be nominated as a candidate for the Federal Legislative Council Elections. However, women were never included in the formal negotiations with the British for Independence and the Malayan Constitution which followed did not guarantee equality for women either.

As for the Chinese women, they were not involved in any mainstream political movement and even though the Malayan Chinese Association was formed in 1949, there was no women's section. The Indians too were not politically motivated but some women did contribute towards the formation of the Malayan Indian Congress in 1946. They were Puan Sri Nahappan and Mrs Lobo. Although the Malayan Indian Congress' Constitution did provide for women's participation at local and state levels, no women's section was formed.

Therefore, it can be said that the Malay women who were politically active during this period generally were from the Malay educated elite group. The reason for this could be that these women belonging to the Malay elite group were the ones with the opportunities of being educated in English schools and exposed to the Western idea of female emancipation.

Women In The Economic Sector During The Colonial Period

Colonialism brought along with it western monopoly capitalism. The simple peasant economy of much of the local Malay community was soon affected by a capitalist orientated market. The introduction of British colonial land policy changed the lives of the peasantry. A new land tenure system, known as the Torrens Land Law, eliminated usufructuary rights. Land became a scarce commodity, sold and owned with registered titles. All unused and uncultivated land automatically became state property. Consequently, access to land became more difficult and the process of proletarization of the peasantry was set in motion. According to historical records, peasant women were more adversely affected than men in terms of losing their access to land.

The British rule attracted many merchant and industrial capitalists to Malaya and these people developed the tin and rubber industries. Large numbers of labourers were brought in from China and India to work in the mines and estates. The Malay community then was still involved in the rural-based subsistence agricultural sector and were disinclined to participate as labourers in commercialized agriculture. However, in due course, with the growth of monetary economy, they were soon drawn into the capitalist fold.

Men no longer could afford to remain in the subsistence agricultural sector but had to sell their labour to the capitalists in exchange for cash in order to sustain their families' livelihood. This involved some degree of out-migration from their villages. Consequently, women had to play a greater role in subsistence production as well as managing the household. But in a capitalist society the term "production" is reserved only for economic activities which can be quantified through monetary exchange in the market, as in the form of wages. Thus, a woman's work, which was not regarded in monetary terms, was not valued though it was indispensable for maintaining the survival of the household. This is the root cause of the downgrading of women's contribution to the economy.

The British implemented the "Divide and Rule" policy to safeguard their hold over Malaya. It was the aim of the policy to keep the three main races segregated from one another and thus preventing the possibility of them uniting and plotting against the British. Hence, the Malays were kept in rural areas, firmly tied to the subsistence sector for the production of rice, the Chinese in the tin mines and the Indians in the rubber estates. From this it can be seen that these deliberate attempts kept the Malays away from the modernizing export-oriented capitalist sector, resulting in them being left behind in the development process.

Just as the men from the indigenous community were retained in the peasant economy, so too were the Malay women. However, their participation rate in both the agricultural and fishing sector had declined in relation to the men's. This can be clearly seen in Table 1.1 and Table 1.2.

Table 1.1
Population Engaged In Padi Cultivation In Malaya, 1911–1957

	Males		Females	
Year	Total	%	Total	%
1911	53,795	49.1	55,679	50.9
1921	262,960	55.7	209,057	44.3
1931	242,436	64.3	134,368	35.7
1947	333,261	70.8	137,378	29.2
1957	264,895	66.5	133,400	33.5

Source: Amarjit Kaur—1989

As seen in Table 1.1, the percentage of women participating in padi cultivation had dropped from 50.9% in 1911 to 33.5% in 1957, whereas the percentage of men in this sector had increased from 49.1% in 1911 to 66.5% in 1957. As will be explained in greater detail in Chapter Two, this was partly due to the capitalist definition of "labour force participation" which under-recorded the actual participation of women. The decrease was also due to the introduction of modern farming methods and the use of modern machinery which displaced the participation of women in agriculture. For example, tasks like weeding or harvesting which were traditionally performed by the womenfolk were taken over by modern technology or by contract male labourers. In general, the European colonizers had little sympathy for maintaining female farmers and all new methods of agriculture were taught to the men only.

Table 1.2
Population Engaged In Fishing In Malaya, 1911–1957

	Males		Females	
Year	Total	%	Total	%
1911	6,216	97.2	177	2.8
1921	48,720	95.2	2,488	4.8
1931	53,551	97.7	1,268	2.3
1947	63,588	98.5	974	1.5
1957	60,669	98.8	762	1.2

Source: Amarjit Kaur—1989

The percentage of women involved in the fishing sector had also decreased from 2.8% in 1911 to 1.2% in 1957. The reason for this could be that a woman's unpaid task such as processing the fish was not accorded economic value and hence, not recorded in the labour force counting.

A point to note is that during this time a minority (5.5%) of the educationally qualified urban-based Malay women were involved in the service sector. Those in the formal service sector were mainly in female-related jobs such as teaching, nursing and midwifery.

In the early nineteenth century, not many Chinese women migrated despite the abundance of Chinese male immigrants. This was because the early male immigrants were reluctant to bring along their families as they themselves had little intention of residing permanently in Malaya. Furthermore, at that time there was the misapprehension that the migration of women was solely for immoral reasons. This stigmatization arose because a few Chinese women who came in the early nineteenth century were mainly involved in prostitution. Due to the disproportionate sex ratio of men and women, these prostitutes filled the vacuum created by the absence of wives. Furthermore, the Chinese, being a patrilineal society, were strongly against the migration of their women for they believed a women's place is at the ancestral home. However, there were some Chinese peasant women who migrated out of necessity to seek a living. These women did not work as prostitutes but instead they worked in tin mines as *dulang* washers or in pepper and gambier estates.

There were two distinct patterns to the Chinese migration; one was based on kinship and the other was based on the "coolie trade". According to the kinship pattern, the immigrants would be brought to Malaya through the aid of his relatives who had already settled there. The "coolie trade" system was for the immigrants who had no means of paying for their passage to Malaya. They would be recruited by labour brokers, or *kheh-taus,* who would pay for their passage. Upon arrival in Malaya, the labour brokers, for a fee, would dispose of these immigrants to employers who needed labour and the immigrant workers would repay their passage from the wages they received.

It was only in the late nineteenth century that the British colonial Government encouraged the large-scale migration of Chinese women with the hope of creating a more stable society through a balanced sex ratio, to lessen sex crimes and to enhance the labour supply. As a result, in the early twentieth century the migration of Chinese women began to increase. Besides the encouragement from the British, the increase was also due to the hard times these women faced in their home country. China, at that time, was badly hit by the economic depression and most of her silk factories had to be closed down, thereby causing severe unemployment. This further induced migration. Thus by 1911 there were already 35,539 Chinese women in Malaya as compared to 15,331 in 1903. Most of them who came, worked in the mines, estates and in construction. In the 1930s, more Chinese women migrated because the Aliens Ordinance of 1933 curbed the migration of Chinese male immigrants but not the females. This made it more expensive for the male to migrate and employers began to prefer hiring Chinese female immigrants instead. Moreover, they were hardworking and less likely to cause trouble. However, in 1938, the Aliens Ordinance was also applied to the women and this curbed the migration of Chinese women.

The Chinese women who came to Malaya were mainly from the lower class of the Chinese feudal-patriachal society and they formed part of the labour force during the colonial period.

The migrant female labour force during the colonial era also comprised of the Indian female immigrants. They were brought in by the British to work mainly in the rubber estates. Since 1796, Indian male immigrants had been brought in to work in the sugar and coffee plantations but their numbers were few. It was only with the growth of the rubber industry in the late nineteenth century that more Indian immigrants were brought in as free or indentured labour.

In 1911, there were 268,269 Indian immigrants and it increased to 470,180 in 1921. However, only 20% out of this number were females. The reason for this was that the Indians were a strong patriarchal-caste society which firmly believed that a woman should depend on a man, thus they were not permitted to travel alone. Furthermore, employers were reluctant to employ female Indian immigrants as it was costly since provisions had to be made for family-based accommodation and maternity needs. However, in the late 1920s, more female Indian immigrants came as this was encouraged by the Government in order to ensure a constant labour supply through stable conjugal units. Encouragement was given in the form of reducing assessment on female workers and increasing the *Kangany's* (middleman) commission for recruiting women workers or married men with their families.

Eighty per cent of the Indian female immigrants were involved in the plantation agriculture sector, working as tappers, weeders or as factory workers in the rubber processing factories. Expectedly, most of them received wages which were much lower than the men's.

During the Japanese Occupation, the rubber and tin industries came to a standstill leaving many Chinese and Indian women jobless. However, Malay women were encouraged by the Japanese to join the labour force. For example, in 1944, the Male Restriction Ordinance was introduced to prohibit men between the ages of 15 to 40 from working in certain areas of employment. Subsequently, a

Women's Employment Bureau was established to direct women into these areas as replacement labour.

After the Second World War, the composition of the labour force changed. With the greater diversification of jobs, women now worked in areas once monopolized by men, for example, in the services and commercial sectors. Nevertheless, these women retained a link with their traditional feminine roles since most of them were employed as teachers or nurses.

Thus, it can be concluded that during the colonial period, with the growth of a capitalistic monetary economy, most of the women's economic contribution had been devalued and under-numerated in the capitalist labour market with the exception of the minority who sold their labour in return for wages. The women included in the labour force count were mainly Chinese and Indian women, the majority of whom worked in the paid sector. The Malay women on the other hand were mainly involved in subsistence agriculture. Their unpaid labour was not accorded any economic value in the national accounting system.

Women And Education During The Colonial Period

Formal education for both sexes in Malaya was first introduced by the British colonial administration. The Straits Settlements were the first to promote formal education. Schools were set up and they were mainly run by Christian missionaries. The first English Language school set up was the Penang Free School in 1816. However, it was only for boys. Then in 1817, the first girls' school was founded as part of the Penang Free School. This school was mainly attended by Europeans, Eurasians, Indians, Chinese, but hardly any Malays. This was because there were not many Malays staying in the Penang urban area and of those who were, did not believe in sending their children to Christian-mission schools, fearing it would undermine the Islamic values and beliefs of their children.

As for the Unfederated Malay States, before the intervention of the British there was no formal education at all other than the *pondok* system of religious education. However, a Malay Sultan or chief could employ a wandering schoolmaster from the Straits Settlements to tutor his sons. Again, women were neglected and not given any formal education. Nevertheless, soon after the signing of the Pangkor Treaty in 1874 the trend of education changed. In 1835, the first Malay boys' school was set up and it was followed with the setting up of an all-Malay girls' school in 1883. Despite this, the number of Malay girls attending school remained small. Many still believed that since a girl's place is at home, she need not be literate to cook, sew or look after her family. Social inhibitions and religious reasons too kept the Malay community from allowing their daughters to attend school.

In addition, the girls' schools that existed then taught subjects that were linked to the traditional role of women as mother and wife. Subjects like craftwork were taught. As for the Malay boys, they were taught industrial skills like animal husbandry or silversmith work as the aim of education then was "to make the son of a fisherman or a peasant a more intelligent fisherman or peasant than his father had been."[1]

Basically, peasants were reluctant to send their children to school as many preferred their children to help in the fields. Thus, those who had the opportunity of being educated were mainly from the aristocratic class and the emerging middle class.

However, in the 1920s, with the encroachment of the capitalist monetary economy, the general attitude of the Malay parents seemed to change slightly for many were becoming aware that a formal education qualification paved the way to better employment opportunities. Steps were taken to improve the Malay vernacular education but this only catered for six years of primary education with no avenues for one to further his studies. Consequently, the Sultan Idris Training College was set up in 1921 at Tanjung Malim to enable selected students from Malay village schools to be trained as Malay schoolmasters. At the same time, the Malay College of Kuala Kangsar was also set up but it was limited to sons of the Malay aristocrats and a few selected students from peasant backgrounds. Its function was to train them to become second level administrators in the colonial administration.

For the women, there was still not much change until the 1930s, when Hajah Zain Suleiman, also known as Ibu Zain, created an awareness on the necessity of formal education for Malay women. Although she met with numerous objections from members of the "Kaum Tua", she also had support from other sections like Ahmad Lufti from the "Kaum Muda". Even then the focus of education was still on religion, handicrafts and domestic skills relevant to the role of women as educator of their children. In line with the then prevailing trend, formal education for women was mainly for the children of the aristocrats and the upper class. The opportunities for boys were greater than for girls and the 1938 statistics reveal that, in the Malay stream, there were 662 boys' schools and only 126 girls' schools.

As for the Indian and Chinese community, most of them attended either the English Government-sponsored or Christian-mission schools or the Chinese and Indian vernacular schools. These vernacular schools had their own syllabus which was based on the school system in their homeland and conducted in their mother tongue. Most of these schools were also financed by Chinese and Indian philanthropists. Quite a number of Chinese women attended vernacular schools as the Chinese community had a tradition which placed high value on literacy education. As for the Indians, the women who attended schools were normally the ones from elite families.

The Japanese Occupation from 1942 to 1944 interrupted the education of many students as most schools were either closed down or made to adopt the Japanese education system with its own syllabus. Furthermore, due to lack of food many children were too sickly to attend school or had to help their parents at subsistence production.

The post-Second World War period brought about significant changes to education. Parents now realized the value of education and the disadvantage of being illiterate in a fast-changing modernizing world. This led to an increase in the number of students who attended school regardless of whether male or female. For example, a perusal of the statistics on percentage of students in school shows that in 1957, 42.6% of the children attending Malay schools were girls, whereas for the English schools, the percentage was 38.85%.

Just before Independence in 1957, the Razak Committee was formed to devise a national system of education whereby there would be common syllabus and textbooks to replace the different systems of education that existed then. It was hoped that this national system of education would help to unite the different ethnic groups which had been separated under the "Divide and Rule" policy of the British. But again, no consideration was given to redress the inequality in women's position to men's in terms of educational attainment.

THE POST-COLONIAL PERIOD

The discussion on this period will include three different historical phases. They are as follows:
1. The intermediate period after Independence, from 1957 to 1970;
2. The post-1970s which spans the period from 1970 to 1980; and
3. The post-1980 period.

In addition to the analysis on the role of women in politics, the economy and in education, there will be a brief discussion on the 1975 Women's Decade and its effect on women in Malaysia.

Just as their British predecessors, the newly formed Government of the Federation of Malaya adopted the philosophy and maxim that "the best Government is the one who governs the least". Thus, the participation of the State in economic activities was kept at a minimum and its role was limited to maintaining law and order in the country, protecting the country from external ingress and providing infrastructural facilities. However, there were efforts by the Government to improve the country's economy and to reduce poverty which was quite widespread. During this period, the Malayan economy was dependent on primary industries (for example, rubber and tin) but in time, due to the vacillating prices of these commodities, emphasis was laid on import-substitution industries instead. Import-substitution industrialization was pursued to generate economic growth and employment opportunities to meet the needs of the expanding labour force. Thus, a changing focus can be detected in the first three development plans. For example, the First Malaya Plan (1956–1960), which was based on the IBRD's (International Bank for Reconstruction and Development) report, placed emphasis on massive rehabilitation programmes for the rubber and tin industries, while the Second Malaya Plan (1961–1965) and the First Malaysia Plan (1966–1970) emphasized industrial growth, the provision of greater employment opportunities and the improvement in the rural standard of living.

Amidst all this emphasis on economic growth, the political situation too underwent a change. "Malaysia" was formed in 1963 and its initial components were Malaya, Singapore, Sabah and Sarawak. However, in 1965, Singapore withdrew from being a component of Malaysia and became an independent country. During this period, there was also growing inequality in the distribution of income. The economy was dominated by foreigners and the Chinese, whereas the majority of Malays were still entrenched in the backward rural subsistence sector, while the Indians were still associated with the plantation or estate sector. Thus, the ownership of wealth was perceived as being concentrated in the hands of foreigners and an immigrant minority while poverty became widespread and was identified with the indigenous race. Ethnic relations among the races soon deteriorated and racial animosity reached its peak in 1969 when racial riots erupted on May 13 of that year. The Government then realized the need to remedy the racial inequalities that existed. As a result, the New Economic Policy (NEP) was launched in 1970. Its two main objectives were to restructure society and to eradicate poverty.

Consequently, in the post-1970 period, there was a breakaway from the *laissez faire* policy. The state had now decided to play an important and immediate role not only in the allocation of resources and the regulation of the economy, but also in the direct ownership of "private capital". This was to be achieved through public enterprises which then would burgeon into the industrial, commercial and agricultural sector. In the industrial sector, stress was no longer given to import-substitution industrialization as it was now regarded unsuitable in view of Malaysia's limited domestic market. Consequently, emphasis was placed on export-oriented industrialization. Under this policy, industries were set up to generate more employment opportunities and to help reduce unemployment as these industries were labour-intensive. The development programmes during this period, that is the Second Malaysia Plan (1971–1975) and the Third Malaysia Plan (1976–1980), had the same aims as the NEP policy, that is to redistribute wealth and eradicate poverty. Gender as an issue, was however, given no mention in any of these plans except for the additional clause in the Third Malaysia Plan (TMP) acknowledging the active participation of women in development and their contribution to the economy. Such an acknowledgement, however, was essentially a gesture in show of support of the United Nation's declaration of the Women's Decade in 1975.

The 1980s marked the beginning of a new trend favouring privatization. Some major Government-controlled entities like the Telecoms Department had been reorganized and privatized. This new policy of privatization denotes a drastic change from the state interventionist policies of the 1970s. Encouragement is now given to the private sector to generate growth and employment with minimal participation from the State. The trend of industrialization has also changed from export-oriented industries to higher technology-based industries in line with Malaysia's aim to achieve the Newly Industrialized Country (NIC) status and to prevent Malaysia's economy from being easily affected by world recession. The two development plans during this decade were the Fourth Malaysia Plan (1981–1985) and the Fifth Malaysia Plan (1986–1990). Both are extensions of the previous plans, bearing the same objectives of restructuring society and eradicating poverty.

Political Development And Women

A detailed analysis of women in politics will be given in Chapter Five but as an overview, it can be stated that, after Independence more women became politically motivated. This awareness was, in part, due to their educational achievements. Education at all levels was encouraged by the Government as its aim was now to develop the nation through human resource development. Education and employment in the paid sector had enabled women to break away from the traditional confines of the home and economic dependence on men. It created a new breed of women who were more sensitive to their surroundings and responsive to the country's needs.

The interest and participation in politics did not arise simultaneously among the women of the different ethnic groups. For instance, between the years 1957 to 1969, it was only the Malay women in contrast to the women of the other ethnic groups who were involved in the political arena yet this was also only to a limited extent. The Kaum Ibu was still merely auxiliary to UMNO, playing the supportive female role. It had only three representatives on the UMNO's Supreme Council as the influence of traditional Malay socio-political culture was still prevalent. Women have always been deemed to play a complementary and supportive role to their menfolk. The members of Kaum Ibu were not consulted in major political matters which were the mainstay of the men. Instead, they were involved only in sectional issues like the economic impoverishment of Malay women or Muslim family law reform. PAS (Parti Angkatan Islam) had also by now started a women's section, the Dewan Muslihat, which had 3,000 members by 1967. However, just like Kaum

Ibu, it still remained a supportive and essentially subordinate political auxiliary.

As for the Chinese and Indian women, there were hardly any attempts made by MCA or MIC to start a women's section during this intermediate period, that is, from 1957 to 1970.

One of the results of the New Economic Policy was that it provided greater opportunity for Malay women to be educated in institutions of higher learning. This led to some significant changes within the Kaum Ibu. For instance, the leadership of Kaum Ibu was gradually taken over by younger and more highly educated Malay women through the encouragement given by male leaders who realized the need for women to be more actively involved in the politics and progress of the Malay people. The name of Kaum Ibu was also eventually changed to Wanita UMNO.

Women of the other ethnic groups too soon realized that they were left out of the political movement. Hence, to ensure that the rights of the women in their ethnic groups would also be protected and to support their male leaders, women sections were soon set up in the respective political parties. In July 1972, the Wanita MCA was formed with Rosemary Chong as its first Chairperson and on July 6, 1975, Wanita MIC was established with Meenambal Arumugal as its leader.

A more detailed analysis of women in politics is given in Chapter Five. Generally, if we compare women in the pre-colonial or colonial days with women now, one can say that women today have made much headway in the political arena in terms of direct participation. Women are now more organized in their demands for political rights. Furthermore, there are now two women Ministers in the Cabinet as compared to one in the first Malaysian Cabinet. Despite the improvement, the role of the majority of women in the political sphere is still restricted to that of a voter and campaigner and the women still do not play a leading part in decision-making. Thus, it can be said that their role in politics is still very much defined within the boundaries of the traditional role of women as supporters in a male-dominated leadership.

Economic Development And Women

A detailed discussion on women in the labour force is provided in Chapter Two but as an introduction it can be said that since 1957, the percentage of women involved in the labour force of the country has increased. Statistics show that the percentage of women in the labour force has increased from 27% in 1957 to 30% in 1970 and to 42.2% in 1984. The reasons behind the increase are varied and this is analysed in Chapter Two, but in general, it can be said that this increase is mainly due to the effect of growing educational opportunities for women and the subsequent "revolution of rising expectations" among educated women. As elaborated in Chapter Two, economic development brought about a greater diversification of employment opportunities. There was a shift in emphasis from primary to secondary industries which created greater job opportunities for women.

The three main sectors in which women are generally involved are the agricultural and the expanding industrial and service sectors. The changing pattern of women's labour force participation in each sector is discussed in detail in Chapter Two. Below is a brief overview of women's involvement in the economy seen from a historical perspective.

Women And Agricultural Development

Agricultural development in Malaysia in the post-Independence era can be divided into two phases, namely, from 1957 until the 1980s, and the National Agricultural Policy (NAP) in 1984 and its implementation period. How the agricultural development process affected women will be discussed within the context of the two phases.

Due to the effects of the Torrens System, land became a commodity in the market. Access to work on the land became more difficult for non-owners and women, as a group with lesser economic and political assets, were deprived of land. In addition, land was frequently divided under the Islamic *faraid* system according to which women were given lesser access. In the post-colonial era, continual emphasis was placed on commercial crop farming and this trend was very much supported by capitalist interests.

This emphasis was apparent in the First Malaya Plan (1956–1960) which favoured large-scale commercialized agriculture. FELDA (Federal Land Development Authority) was formed in 1956 with the objective of increasing the commercial production of rubber and palm oil. This objective was also evident in the First Malaysia Plan (1966–1970) although it was not given as much prominence. This is discernible from the fact that credit facilities, offered by the new marketing agency, the Federal Agricultural Marketing Authority (FAMA), were open to both small and large scale producers. However, the Government did not realize that these policies would only cause a widening in the inequalities between the poorer and the better-off strata of the peasantry. The social unheaval which broke out in 1969 soon made this situation evident.

In the 1960s, the Government adopted the Green Revolution programme, introduced by the Western powers with the purpose of increasing the output from the agricultural sector. To achieve this purpose, new irrigation systems were built and old ones improved, better seeds, new crops of better yielding varieties and fertilizers were provided, trained personnels were also sent to teach new farming methods to the farmers.

However, as detailed in Chapter Two, these programmes were advantageous to the men farmers and not to the women farmers. Emphasis on rural development, especially in terms of eradication of poverty, was frequently associated with developing better farmers. Women, however, were not considered farmers in their own rights but were referred to as "farmers' wives". Under the development plans, the traditional farming system was gradually replaced with modern methods such as the use of machines and fertilizers. Various irrigation schemes were carried out in places like Kemubu in Kelantan, Sg Muda in Kedah and Sg Manik in Perak. More Government agencies like LPN (Lembaga Padi Negara) were set up to help train farmers and market their produce. FELDA too opened up more land and set up various settlements.

Amidst all these development programmes to improve and increase the agricultural production, the role of women as farmers declined. As mentioned earlier, women have always participated in the agricultural sector even in the pre-colonial era. However, their percentage share in agriculture declined steadily in the post-Independence period. This can be attributed to three main reasons. Firstly, the modernization of agriculture in the post-Independence era which benefited men rather than women. In this process, men rather than women were encouraged to participate actively in market-oriented agriculture. Women, on the other hand, were relegated to domestic production. All new methods of farming and marketing were only taught to the men. Even rural-based organizations backed by the Government, like KEMAS and FELDA, wittingly or otherwise, discriminated against women farmers by providing them courses only on nutrition, tailoring, handicraft and home economics. This attitude could be a legacy of the influence of the European colonizers who considered farming cultivation a better vocation for men than for women. Secondly, as mentioned earlier, mechanization had taken over a woman's job in planting, harvesting and threshing, thus making women's labour redundant. Thirdly, urban-based industrialization in the 1970s had lured women, especially the young and unmarried, to migrate from agricultural to non-agricultural sectors. All these factors account for the steady decline in the percentage of women involved in the agricultural sector.

The next phase in agricultural development is the present phase which began in 1984 with the implementation of the National Agricultural Policy (NAP). NAP's objective is to revitalize the agriculture sector and maximize the income from agriculture through the consolidation and efficient utilization of resources and the increased contribution of the sector to the overall economic development of the country. Development efforts have been geared towards modernization and consolidation of the unorganized smallholders sector. Since women have been dislocated from the rural peasant sector and generally do not control land assets, they are therefore, handicapped in participating equally in this new agriculture phase.

Women And Industrial Development

Besides working towards a politically stable country, the newly elected Government in 1957 also aimed for rapid economic growth to finance development programmes.

The Pioneer Industries Ordinance was passed in 1958 to encourage the establishment of import-substitution industries. It provided incentives like tax reliefs. The import-substitution industries generated small-scale engineering spin-offs in urban areas but it also produced an over-concentration of capital-intensive industries which could not absorb an adequate proportion of the nation's rapidly growing workforce. Furthermore, it also did not make much use of local raw materials and was heavily controlled by foreign owners. Due to all these weaknesses, the Government turned to export-oriented industrialization as a development strategy.

This change occurred in the 1970s after the NEP policy had been implemented. However, some emphasis had already been placed on export-oriented industrialization even before the NEP policy was promulgated in 1970. For example, the Pioneer Industries Ordinance was replaced in 1968 by the Investment Incentive Act which gave priority to export-oriented industries. This provided a lot of incentives to encourage foreign investments. They came in a package form of free trade zone facilities, generous tax incentives, flexible labour regulations and labour law restrictions on trade-union formations. The first Free Trade Zone was opened at Bayan Lepas, on Penang Island, to encourage the relocation of offshore sourcing industries. The development plans, like the Third Malaysia Plan (1976–1980) too, placed heavy emphasis on export-oriented industrialization. Soon there was a major growth in industries like electronics, food processing, plastics, textiles and garments.

The export-oriented industries had succeeded in generating greater employment opportunities as it was labour-intensive. However, this increase in job opportunities was mainly for women workers and it resulted in the massive entry of women into the manufacturing sector. For example, in 1957, the percentage of women in the manufacturing sector was 17% but it soon increased to 29% in 1970 and 39.5% in 1980. On the other hand, the percentage of men in the manufacturing workforce had declined from 83% in 1957 to 71% in 1970 and 60.5% in 1980. This was due to the fact that the majority of the new industries favoured female more than male labour. This is based on the assumption that factory jobs are more suited to women's gender abilities. For example, the work requires abilities like keen eye-sight, manual dexterity and the ability to sit for long hours. These abilities are usually associated with the female gender. Women workers are also more willing to accept the lower wages paid by these industries compared to the men. Furthermore, most women job-seekers in this period were educated but found it difficult to acquire jobs in the preferred feminine occupations like nursing or teaching and since factory jobs were in abundance, it was, therefore, expected of them to join this sector. In addition, the NEP had encouraged Malay rural-urban migration and many of the young girls who migrated were readily absorbed into the manufacturing sector. It is also asserted by some writers (for example, Heyzer, 1982) that the development process had caused an impoverishment of the rural peasantry. This forced poor households to release their daughters from the land to work in industries so as to sustain their families' survival.

In the 1980s, Malaysia re-evaluated its dependence on export-oriented industries. This was because Malaysia had been badly hit by the world recession as export-oriented industries rely heavily on world demand. Thus, when demand fell, the earnings from these industries were drastically reduced and retrenchment among industrial workers became rampant. Around this time too, Malaysia had started on a heavy-industries programme. Unfortunately, the Heavy Industry Corporation Of Malaysia (HICOM) failed to take off effectively as there were a lot of problems in its initial implementation (for example, managerial mistakes, etc) and its failure resulted in an additional burden to the country's external debt. (It has however proved to be a successful venture by the late l980s).

Therefore, in the 1980s, Malaysia revised its industrial policies to focus on resource-based, higher-technology industrialization. This is explained in the Industrial Master Plan Report. These industries will be more capital-intensive needing less unskilled labour. It is expected that such industries will use more male rather than female labour. This is because most women workers, unlike the men, do not possess technical skills. As such, unless there is concerted action to produce more technically-oriented women workers, it is predicted that there will soon be a decline in the female component of the manufacturing sector's labour force (see Jamilah, 1989).

Women And Service Sector Development

When women began to leave the subsistence agriculture sector, many of them went into the service sector. This trend was most noticeable after Independence. Their percentage of involvement in this sector increased from 11.6% in 1957 to 14.8% in 1970 and reached 19.4% in 1980.

Details on the service sector are found in Chapter Two but briefly, it can be said that job activities in the service sector can be divided into three types, namely, old services, complementary services and new services.

As analysed in Chapter Two, the emergence of these types of services seem to relate closely with three phases in the country's economic development. Firstly, in the period between 1957 and 1970 when the Malaysian economy was still dependent on primary industries (for example, agriculture), most women worked in the old services activities employed mainly as domestic servants. During this period, the service sector was the second most important sector for women's employment after agriculture. Secondly, when Malaysia turned to promoting secondary industries and manufacturing in the 1970s, the trend began to change. Besides working in the industrial sector women were also more involved in the newly emerging complementary services like banking, finance, transportation, wholesale and retail. For example, their percentage in the complementary services rose from 5.2% in 1970 to 12.7% in 1980. Thirdly, now in the 1980s, the new services occupations have incorporated more women. Of all the sub-industries in the new services, the most important ones are education and public administration.

Education Reforms And Women

Besides instilling the necessity of education and the advantage of literacy among the people, the education system has been upgraded and tailored to produce a more scientific and technically-minded nation. In 1960, the education system was reviewed and a few changes were made. The Rahman Talib Committee expanded technological and vocational education besides introducing vocational subjects like Industrial Arts, Commerce and Agriculture Science for boys and Home Science for girls. These so-called prevocational subjects chosen for each sex reflects the gender orientation of the curriculum which perpetuates the ordained role of a woman as a housewife, mother and educator of her children. These values fostered by the State are in tune with the Malaysian community values. As detailed in Chapter Three, even until the present time most women students in tertiary institutions are in the Arts Stream rather than in the Science and with a noticeable minority in the Engineering field.

Notwithstanding these traditional orientations, the percentage of girls enrolled in all levels of education has increased, especially in the upper levels of education. As will be elaborated in Chapter Three, the 1960s marked the expansion of educational opportunities and the rapid entry of women into schools and by the 1970s, its cumulative effect was manifested in the large numbers of women at institutions of higher learning and their subsequent entry into the job market. In 1979, the Cabinet Committee reviewed the education system and introduced the KBSR for primary students and KBSM for secondary students. For the KBSM system, a new subject called "Living Skills" was introduced to replace the former prevocational subjects. Skills like agriculture, industrial skills, commerce and home science are now available to both sexes. It is now left to be seen whether parents will encourage their daughters to break away from gender-based education streaming.

Women's Decade And Its Effect On Malaysian Women

In 1975, the Women's Decade was declared by the United Nations (UN). The Decade was to take effect from 1976 to 1985 and its theme was "Equality of Rights, Development and Peace". The main objective of this declaration was to instill in all countries the need to value the role and upgrade the status of women in society. Thus, countries which recognized this declaration was to plan actions at district, national and international levels to achieve this aim.

Just like the other UN members, Malaysia too recognized this declaration and made efforts to integrate women into the development process of our country. The Government has shown its support through allocating funds and setting up organizations. One of the steps taken was the setting up of the National Advisory Council on the Integration of Women in Development (NACIWID). The purpose of this council was to advise the Government on women-related matters in development. Subsequently, in 1982, the Women Affairs Secretariat was set up in the Prime Minister's Department to administer affairs relating to women. The Government has also made allocation of funds in the Third Malaysia Development Plan for development of women mainly in their primary role as housewives, mothers and supplementary income earners. These funds were channelled through organizations like the National Family Planning and Development Board or the ministry dealing with social welfare. Besides this, the Government service has provided opportunities for educated women to be promoted to high positions in Government departments and organizations which previously were monopolized by men. Laws to upgrade the status of women, for example, equality in pay for men and women in the Government service sector, have also been legislated. A National Policy for Women was constructed in December 1989. Its contents will be incorporated into the Sixth Malaysia Plan (1990–1995).

CONCLUSION

Together with the historical development of the nation, the role and status of women have encountered much change. A perusal of the historical development of our country reveals that the role of women which was once confined to the domestic domain has now been extended to the public domain. This can be witnessed from the increased participation of women in politics, the economy and in education. Colonization and capitalistic economic development have devalued women's unpaid economic participation and fostered the "housewife ideology". However, rapid economic development in the post-colonial era and the promotion of education at all levels are the two determining factors that have brought about the growing emancipation of women. Women's contribution to the development of the nation is now actively encouraged and acknowledged by the State.

NOTES

[1] Maxwell (1920).
[2] Refer Cheong Siew Yoong (1983).

2
Women's Productive Role And Labour Force Participation

Whether out in the open fields, the plantations, the tin mines, in the plush confines of the office, in the sweltering factories or even at home, Malaysian women have always been contributing tangibly to the economy. Their involvement in the nation's economy is either direct or indirect, and in the form of paid or unpaid labour. But due to the inadequacies inherent in the definition of workforce or the accounting of those in the labour force, women's economic contribution has been generally under-represented. A look at this definition will reveal these inadequacies. The concept of "workforce" as formulated by the Statistics Department is very much influenced by the Neo-classical Economics' definition of "work". Emphasis is given to exchange-value rather than to use-value and therefore defines workforce as "people who are either at work or are seeking work." In Peninsular Malaysia, workforce or labour force refers to those who, during the reference week were in the 15–64 years age group and who were either employed or unemployed as defined [refer to endnotes for the full definition].[1] According to this definition, persons working without pay are regarded as "outside the labour force." This then would imply that child-rearing and the domestic work of the housewife are considered as not possessing any economic value. This also means that women's unpaid labour in the economic sector would be grossly under-valued. The limited definition of "work" also excludes the economic contribution of housewives who produce for domestic consumption as well as for the market and of many women who are self-employed, and those who tend to work seasonally and sporadically. In conclusion, the nature and pattern of women's work cannot be covered by the given definition. Thus, the aim of this chapter is to:

1. Provide a true account of women's actual contribution to the nation's economy;
2. Trace the general trends and patterns of women's participation in the labour force;
3. Highlight the sectors in which women are concentrated; and
4. To suggest possible steps to be taken to improve women's position and status in the labour force.

WOMEN'S CONTRIBUTION TO THE NATION'S ECONOMY

As analysed in Chapter One, since pre-colonial times, Malaysian women have played an intrinsic role in the village economy. Engaged in subsistence agriculture, they worked alongside the menfolk. The family functioned as the basic economic unit.[2] Though there existed a traditional allocation of tasks based on gender whereby the men and women had their own clearly defined spheres of influence, both played a direct, productive and valued role in the economy. Coupled with this productive role, women carried out the tasks of child-rearing and running a home simultaneously. But with the process of colonialism came capitalism and the commercialization of agriculture which altered the productive conditions of the pre-colonial society. Labour became a marketable commodity[3] and production for sale took on greater importance as compared to subsistence production. These changes in the relations of production also brought about some changes in gender relations. The demarcation between commodity production and domestic labour became all the more clear-cut causing a separation of labour based on gender, that is, men getting involved in commodity production while women were left to carry out domestic chores. Women were progressively confined to the home front as their direct participation in the market economy declined. Even their reproductive role and their domestic labour were not given their due monetary value. This trend continued even in post-colonial times. Industrialization only helped perpetuate this gender-based subordination of women. When women went out to work in the factories, they were mostly employed in labour-intensive jobs which were considered inferior to the men's and given lower pay. Their workload was assessed as being of lesser importance to the males and their wages were viewed by employers in the private sector as supplementary to the men's.

A survey conducted by the Ministry of Labour and Manpower revealed that:

> In 1980, the average monthly wage rate paid to female workers were between $9 and $209 less than that paid to male workers in similar occupations. The position was, however, an improvement, though marginal, compared with the differential, in 1974 of between $27 and $243. (Treasury, *Economic Report 1982/1983*).

Thus modernization did not change much the gender-specific job situation. Men's and women's work is still very much defined by gender ideologies. [4] Till today, there exists an artificial separation between the productive and reproductive labour of women. A consequence of this is that the private domestic sphere of women is separated from the public social sphere of men thus limiting women's access to the market and outside resources. Much of women's work is hidden within the informal economy and in the home and hence not officially recorded and under-valued.[5] Yet, even within the given limited definition of "workforce", we see the growing participation and contribution of women in the nation's economy.

TRENDS AND PATTERNS OF WOMEN'S PARTICIPATION IN THE LABOUR FORCE

On attaining political independence, Malaysia's development planning gave priority to the need for overall economic growth. Malaysia has since achieved rapid economic development. By 1984, her per capita gross national product (GNP) stood at US$1,980, the result of an average annual growth rate of 4.3% during the period 1960–84.[6] This economic development process brought about significant structural changes in production and employment. For example, there has been a major shift from the primary to the secondary sector, that is, from the traditional sector of subsistence farming to the modern sector characterized by production of marketable goods. Hence, there has been a rapid increase in manufacturing activities and the growth of resource-based and labour-intensive industries.[7]

As a result of this, the participation of women in the Malaysian economy has, in the last three decades, shown a marked increase. The process of industrialization and urbanization has also played a vital role in determining the pattern of female labour force participation. It has shifted from a concentration in subsistence rural economy to a greater involvement in the urban industrial sector and the service sector, making women's contribution to the economy all the more visible and concrete. Three main factors can be attributed to this changing trend in women's economic participation, that is:

1. The rapid expansion of educational facilities which has led to the modernization of women, changed their attitude towards paid employment, improved their skills and thus increased their employability as well as their earning capacity;
2. The rapid economic development and industrialization and the corresponding expansion of the urban economy have created new job opportunities for women especially in the labour-intensive industries such as textiles and electronics; and
3. The implementation of the NEP. The two main objectives of this policy, that is, to eradicate poverty and to restructure Malaysian society have facilitated greater social and spatial mobility and the transition from rural to urban-based activities, from unpaid to paid employment.

Besides these three main factors, the increase in female participation rates in the labour force has also been effected by the delayed age of marriage and the reduction of fertility. This has reduced the life-cycle phase associated with child-care responsibilities thus allowing women more opportunity to seek paid employment. Added to this, the advancement in technology has reduced the demand for hard physical labour whilst increasing the pleasantness of the work environment. This in turn poses a greater attraction of the labour market for women. Also the high cost of urban living has caused the gradual erosion of traditional reservations. Women now see the need to seek for paid employment outside the home. Half of Malaysia's population consists of women and out of this, 44% are involved in the labour force as compared to 87% of men.[9] Figure 2.1 provides information on the labour force participation by sex and age group for the years 1957, 1970, 1980 and 1984. From Table 2.1, we can see that the female labour force participation rates (LFPRs) showed a steady increase during those years. From 30.8% in 1957, it then rose to 36.3% in 1970, 39.3% in 1980 and 43.9% in 1984.

A comparison of male and female participation pattern in Figure 2.1 indicates that the LFPR gap between the sexes has been closing-in since the post-war era. Though it is apparent that the males always had a higher participation rate as compared to females, yet the female LFPR experienced a more dramatic change. The M-shaped, bi-modal curves for female LFPR manifest the following:

1. That the 1957 age curve has a low first peak at age group 20–24, and a second higher peak at age group 45–49; the higher female LFPRs in the older age groups are typical in agrarian-based economies.
2. That the 1980 age curve has a pronounced sharp peak at the age group 20–24, and a second lower peak at the age group 40–44 and shows a significant rise as a whole.[10]

Figure 2.2 shows female labour force participation by ethnicity in Peninsular Malaysia. A breakdown of female age-participation profile by ethnic groups reveals that the participation rates of the various ethnic groups are converging at the younger age categories. This suggests that cultural and religious factors inhibiting the labour force participation of younger women are declining in importance. Simultaneously, this participation seems to be more acutely affected by economic and educational factors.[11] The employment status of females can be classified into four main categories, that is, employers, employees, own-account workers and unpaid family workers. The trend in the past two decades, 1960–1980, has been towards an increase in wage employment with a decline in the proportion of unpaid family workers and own-account workers. Women have been absorbed into the employment structure rather unevenly across sectors and along the occupational hierarchy as indicated by Tables 2.2 and 2.3.[12] Information collected over the years confirmed that men still predominate in the higher echelons of the job hierarchies, as shown by Figure 2.3. In the waged sector, women continue to predominate in occupations identified with femininity such as clerical, nursing, teaching and services.

Figure 2.1
Male And Female Labour Force Participation Rates For Peninsular Malaysia

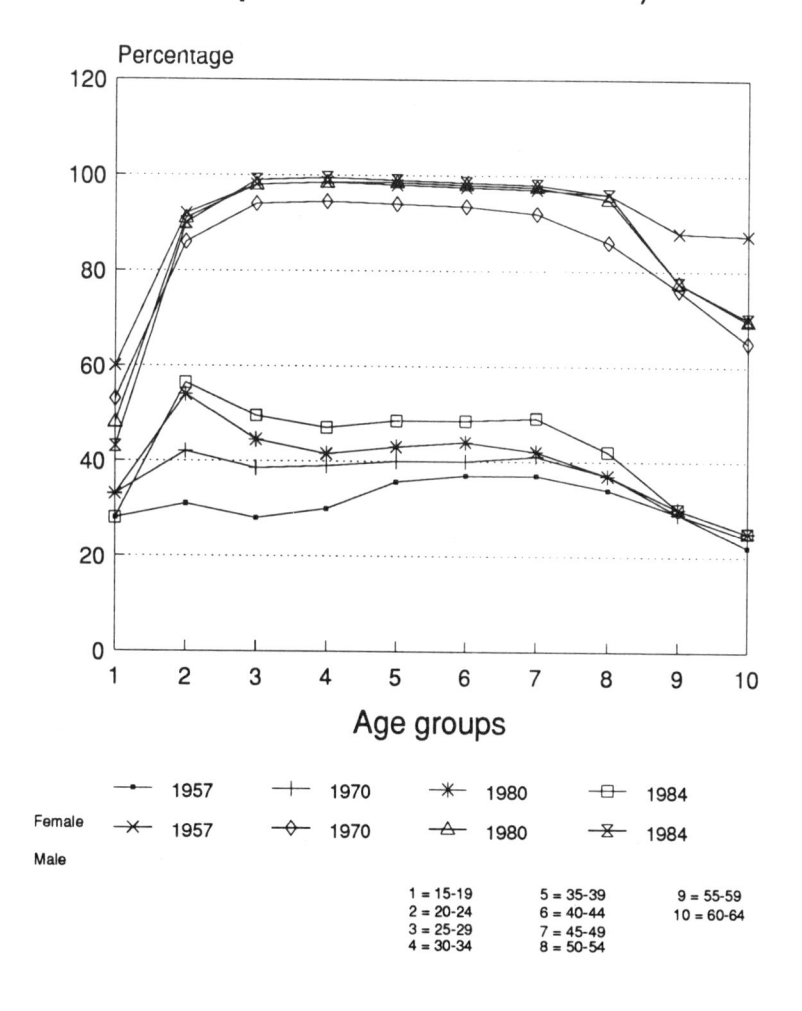

Female							
—•— 1957	—+— 1970	—*— 1980	—□— 1984				

Male
—×— 1957 —◇— 1970 —△— 1980 —✕— 1984

1 = 15-19   5 = 35-39   9 = 55-59
2 = 20-24   6 = 40-44   10 = 60-64
3 = 25-29   7 = 45-49
4 = 30-34   8 = 50-54

Source: Constructed from Siti Rohani (1989), Table 10.

Figure 2.2
Female Labour Force Participation By Ethnicity For Peninsular Malaysia

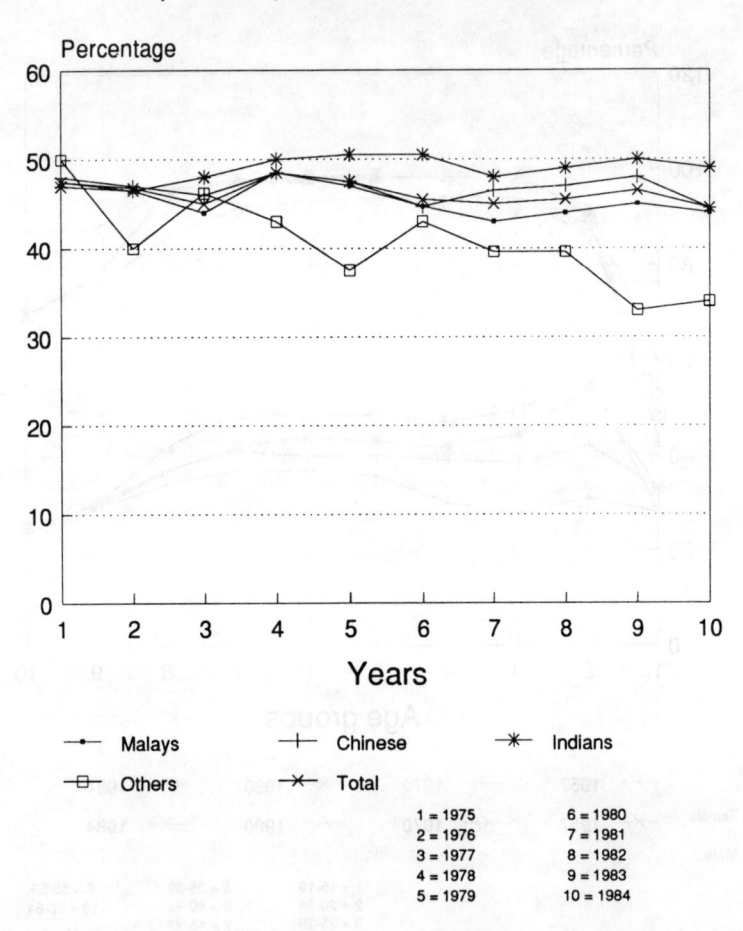

- Malays
- Chinese
- Indians
- Others
- Total

1 = 1975　　6 = 1980
2 = 1976　　7 = 1981
3 = 1977　　8 = 1982
4 = 1978　　9 = 1983
5 = 1979　　10 = 1984

Source: Constructed from Siti Rohani (1989), Table 11.

LABOUR FORCE PARTICIPATION 37

Figure 2.3
Distribution Of Employed Persons By Sex And Occupation

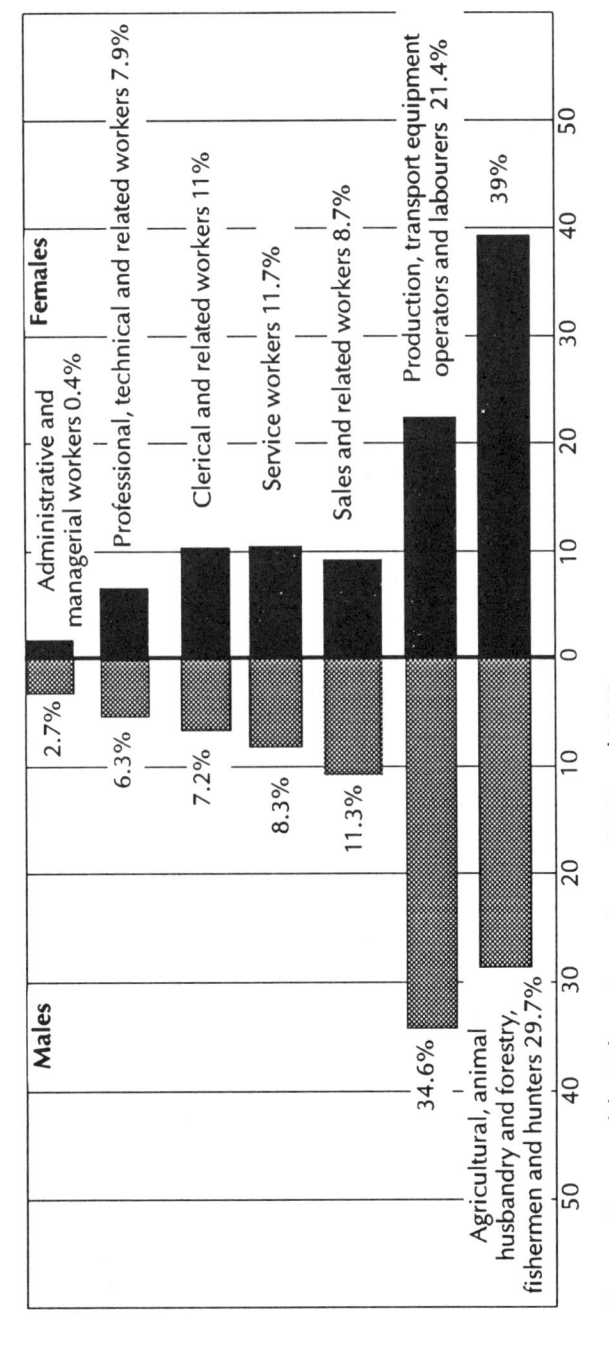

Females
- Administrative and managerial workers 0.4%
- Professional, technical and related workers 7.9%
- Clerical and related workers 11%
- Service workers 11.7%
- Sales and related workers 8.7%
- Production, transport equipment operators and labourers 21.4%
- Agricultural, animal husbandry and forestry, fishermen and hunters 39%

Males
- Administrative and managerial workers 2.7%
- Professional, technical and related workers 6.3%
- Clerical and related workers 7.2%
- Service workers 8.3%
- Sales and related workers 11.3%
- Production, transport equipment operators and labourers 34.6%
- Agricultural, animal husbandry and forestry, fishermen and hunters 29.7%

Source: *Report of the Labour Force Survey, 1980 and 1983.*

Table 2.1
Labour Force Participation Rate By Sex And Age-Group For Peninsular Malaysia For 1957, 1970, 1980 and 1984

Age-Group	1957	1970	1980	1984
Females				
10 – 14	7.4	7.7	5.4	–
15 – 19	27.9	33.0	33.5	28.2
20 – 24	31.2	41.9	54.0	56.2
25 – 29	27.7	38.4	44.6	49.4
30 – 34	30.5	39.0	40.5	46.1
35 – 39	34.2	40.0	42.7	48.0
40 – 44	35.3	40.0	43.8	47.8
45 – 49	36.3	40.7	41.4	48.8
50 – 54	33.7	36.6	36.5	41.6
55 – 59	29.4	29.2	30.8	31.2
60 – 64	22.3	23.7	25.0	24.9
15 – 64	30.8	36.3	39.3	43.9
Males				
10 – 14	9.6	9.0	7.9	–
15 – 19	60.0	52.3	47.9	43.1
20 – 24	92.7	87.1	91.1	90.4
25 – 29	97.5	93.5	92.4	98.2
30 – 34	97.9	94.4	98.0	98.8
35 – 39	97.7	94.0	98.2	98.7
40 – 44	97.2	93.2	97.7	98.3
45 – 49	96.2	91.5	96.6	97.8
50 – 54	93.7	86.7	92.7	93.8
55 – 59	88.4	75.6	77.4	76.9
60 – 64	87.6	65.2	68.6	69.3
15 – 64	90.0	83.4	86.6	86.5

Source: Population and Housing Census data for 1957, 1970 and 1980. For 1984, Labour Force Survey Report, December 1987.

Table 2.2
Percentage Distribution Of Female Employment By Sector In Peninsular Malaysia From 1975–1986

	[1]	[2]	[3]	[4]	[5]	[6]	[7]
1975	50.3	0.4	17.0	0.9	0.1	0.7	30.6
1979	43.8	0.4	19.9	0.9	0.3	1.0	33.6
1980	40.2	0.4	20.7	1.0	0.2	1.0	36.4
1981	37.6	0.3	21.8	1.3	0.3	1.3	37.4
1982	33.4	0.4	22.1	1.3	0.1	1.0	41.7
1983	30.9	0.5	23.4	1.5	0.0	1.0	42.7
1984	29.9	0.3	22.4	1.3	0.1	1.2	44.8
1985	28.9	0.3	21.9	1.3	0.0	1.4	46.2
1986	27.5	0.3	22.5	1.0	0.0	1.2	47.5

[1] Agriculture
[2] Mining and quarrying
[3] Manufacturing
[4] Construction
[5] Electricity, gas, water and sanitary services
[6] Transportation, storage and communication
[7] Services

Source: From various Labour Force Reports from 1962–1986.

Table 2.3
Female Employment By Occupational Status In Peninsular Malaysia From 1975–1986

	[1]	[2]	[3]	[4]	[5]	[6]	[7]	Total
1975	5.6	0.1	7.4	8.0	10.7	50.0	18.2	100
1976	6.0	0.1	7.9	8.0	11.1	46.4	20.5	100
1977	6.3	0.2	8.3	7.8	10.8	45.8	20.8	100
1978	5.9	0.2	8.4	8.0	11.2	45.6	20.7	100
1979	6.6	0.2	9.8	8.3	11.6	42.8	20.7	100
1980	7.9	0.4	11.0	8.7	11.7	39.0	21.4	100
1981	8.2	0.3	12.2	8.4	12.0	36.3	22.6	100
1982	8.3	0.5	13.3	9.1	13.5	33.8	21.6	100
1983	8.2	0.6	14.1	9.6	13.5	31.1	22.9	100
1984	9.4	0.6	14.9	10.4	14.1	29.7	20.9	100
1985	9.6	0.6	15.3	11.3	14.2	28.7	20.3	100
1986	10.1	0.8	14.8	11.0	15.1	27.3	21.0	100

[1] Professional, technical and related workers
[2] Administrative and managerial workers
[3] Clerical and related workers
[4] Sales and related workers
[5] Service workers
[6] Agricultural, animal husbandry and forestry, fishermen and hunters
[7] Production, transport equipment operators and labourers.

Source: From various Labour Force Reports from 1962–1986.

The sectors of the economy which women are concentrated in are somewhat different from the men's in terms of characteristics, opportunities afforded, wage, status, security, etc.[13] The following section will take a look at women's participation in four major sectors of the economy, namely agriculture, business, manufacturing and services.

FEMALE EMPLOYMENT BY SECTOR

Table 2.2 provides a summary of the sectoral distribution of the female workforce from 1975 to 1986. Table 2.3 shows female employment by occupational status in Peninsular Malaysia.

Women In The Agricultural Sector

In the early years soon after Independence, the nation's development plans emphasized an agro-based economy and the women's participation rate in the agricultural sector rose. But the implementation of the development plans in the 1970s saw the fast expansion of the manufacturing and service sectors' activities which absorbed women into the workforce at a much faster and higher rate. This resulted in a decline in the percentage rate of the female involvement in agriculture. In 1957, as revealed by data from the population census available for Peninsular Malaysia, 77% of females were employed in the agricultural sector. By 1980, their participation rate had dropped to 43%.[14] As indicated in Table 2.2, the percentage distribution of female employment in the agricultural sector has since gently declined. The rural women's participation in agriculture is generally ignored. Much of their work is in the form of unpaid labour and thus not considered as economic activity. The advent of technology and modernization has not helped the rural women's situation. Rural development programmes and subsequent agricultural mechanization have reduced poverty but at the same time they have brought about a significant reduction in labour utilization both for men and women. Yet it was the women who were more adversely affected.[15] Their labour was largely displaced by modern technology and in some cases replaced by men.[16] Jobs previously jointly undertaken by men and women such as harvesting, have been taken over by the men only while women have been receding into their domestic sphere, becoming full-time housewives. This is the rural "housewifization" process, an indirect outcome of past agricultural development policies. This has sharpened the distinction between the productive and reproductive role of the women, and the distinction between male producers and female reproducers. State organizations too, whether consciously or not, have, until lately, discriminated against women. Within rural development agencies separate organizations were set up for men and women. While the men's organizations handled business affairs such as marketing and subsidies, the women's emphasized activities such as tailoring and home-management. Membership in farm organizations which offered training and education in new technology was mostly male.[17] This ideological distinction between male producers and female reproducers has cost the rural women a loss in their economic base. Though they continued to be vitally involved in agricultural production, they were until lately primarily perceived as housewives, for example, FELDA (Federal Land Development Authority) women are still viewed as "wives of settlers".[18] This implies that they play a subsidiary role to their husbands in developing the land. In fact the women have always been farmers and settlers in their own right. A consequence of the housewife ideology is the decreased access of rural women to agricultural resources, education, employment and social benefits as evinced by the fact that women own only 11% of the total land and they do not own the various farm machinery and assets.[19] Thus it appears that the process of development has not improved the economic position of the rural women.

Women In Business

There are several chambers of commerce and industry and trade associations established in Malaysia but they are mainly dominated by the male business community. The existing women social organizations on the other hand are welfare-oriented, seeing to the needs of battered women and other such needy groups. Thus there is a lack of trade and business associations to meet the needs of our businesswomen. Presently there is only one recently created trade association established for Malay businesswomen, that is, Persatuan Perniagaan Wanita Bumiputra (Perniagawati)[20] and an association for women professionals in management.

In the history of our development it is quite apparent that in the 1960s, as well as the 1970s, no specific attention or incentives were offered to encourage women participation in business.

Though the 1980s saw a greater awareness of the role of women in development, yet there hardly seems to be any specific provision for the integration of women into the economic development process.[21] It was only recently in late 1990 that more positive steps were taken as exemplified by the recent Budget which provides for substantial separate income tax exemptions for working women. The recent proliferation of cooperatives established and run by women to meet their credit needs, reflects women's inaccessibility to established credit and loan facilities on account of their gender status. [22]

The distribution of employed females by occupational status as indicated in Table 2.3 shows that the proportion of women in managerial and executive positions has not changed much, remaining consistently at less than 1%. Malaysia still has very few women entrepreneurs. Women in business can be classified as employers, self employed and own account workers. In 1984, 0.6% of Malaysian women entrepreneurs were classified as employers, while 16% were classified as own-account workers. Hardly 10% of the total number of all employers were women.[23] Women can be regarded as a minority group and business proprietorship offers an individual in this group the means to assimilate herself with the majority, that is, the men, and to attain a degree of equality. The more popular areas for female proprietors are self-employed, small-scale trades, services and industries. Generally, women who are active in independent trading, have few alternative means of earning a living. This is usually due to lack of skills or training that prevents them from venturing into other types of enterprises.

CURRENT STATUS OF WOMEN MANAGERS

In Malaysia, women at corporate managerial levels are primarily involved in service industries (for e.g. public relations, management consultancy, communications, etc.). Eighty per cent of the companies in which women are involved are publicly listed. A project conducted by the Asian Institute of Management (AIM) in 1987 found that 90% of Malaysian businesswomen are in their 30s, and 70% were married. Three-quarters of them reported English as their second language; 70% had university degrees and about 15% had postgraduate education while 35% had received academic honours and scholarships.[24] Some of the problems faced by these women are sex discrimination, the lack of facilities in training and career counselling within their companies, the sense of being hampered by a lack of technical skills and the added burden of domestic responsibilities. Basically these women enjoy their jobs, finding in them a sense of fulfilment. They credit their success to supportive bosses, hard work and perseverance.

CURRENT STATES OF WOMEN ENTREPRENEURS

A study carried out by a team of researchers at Universiti Malaya as part of an Asean-wide study found that 40% of the 110 female entrepreneur participants were in their 30s while 30% were in their 40s. A large percentage were married, that is, 60%, while 20% were unmarried singles. Compared to the women managers, the educational attainment of women entrepreneurs is very different. Less than 25% had university degrees while less than 5% had post-graduate education. Eighteen per cent of these women entrepreneurs were involved in retail trade and 40% were involved in service industries like insurance, community services, recreational services, etc. Out of the 110 women involved in this study, 60% were in sole control of their enterprises. Many were involved in hawking, retailing and wholesaling for these do not require large capital outlays. More than half of them expressed the need for self-improvement in areas of marketing and finance as well as management activities and planning. These with the expected problem of balancing their home and career responsibilities were their main concerns.

WOMEN IN THE MANUFACTURING SECTOR

With the New Economic Policy (NEP), industrialization became one of the major component in leading the nation's economic growth. Export-oriented industrialization was emphasized and vigorously pursued from the 1970s to the mid-1980s. The manufacturing sector grew rapidly. In the 1970s, the average annual growth rate was 12.5%. This allowed for the entry of men and women in increasing numbers into the labour force. This swift economic development accompanied by structural transformation, plus the fact that Malaysian women do not face serious social-cultural norms prohibiting them from participating in paid employment, has created the trend of women's increasing participation in urban-industrial employment. Consequently, there has been a massive rural-urban migration of young women, especially young Malay women.

Since the 1970s, the female's rate of absorption into the manufacturing sector has been faster than the male's. The effects of internationalization of production reached Malaysia in the mid-1960s. This entailed the growth of "off-shore factories" involved in labour-intensive manufacturing for export, that is, industries such as electronics, clothing and textiles. Despite "non-gender specific" development planning, the establishment of these export-oriented industries created more job opportunities for women than for men, since women suited the demands of these industries, that is, keener eye-sight, manual dexterity and the ability to sit for long hours on the factory bench doing intricate work under strict supervision. Studies have shown that under these conditions, women's productivity is higher than men's. Moreover, women are less daunted by the low wages accorded them by these industries. Although it can be argued that the manufacturing sector has provided massive job opportunities for women thus allowing them greater economic independence yet the position of women in these new forms of employment must be assessed. These jobs are characterized by their low wages, long hours, tedious work, health hazards and the lack of upward occupational mobility. Also, these industries are volatile industries, that is, highly susceptible to sharply fluctuating demands for their products thus affecting job stability.[26] Women workers in these industries face a constant threat of retrenchment. The question that arises is whether women are getting a "fair deal" for their participation in this export-oriented industrialization programme? This query becomes all the more urgent considering the fact that women workers form the backbone of some of the major industries upon which the Malaysian manufacturing sector of the 1970s and 1980s is premised, that is, electronics, clothing and textiles. Malaysia, as an open economy, was adversely affected by the world recession and experienced a period of recession from 1982 until 1986. This experience influenced the Government's decision to change her industrial policy. Now the trend is towards "industrial deepening" with emphasis on heavy and resource-based industries with upstream and downstream linkage effects.[27] The Government's aim to achieve the status of a "Newly Industrialized Country" has encouraged the entry of higher-technology industries. Women workers in the manufacturing sector are adversely affected by these changes since higher-technology industries demand technical skills from their workers. Because women are generally unskilled workers and since there has been a general shift from labour-intensive to higher capital-intensive industries, women workers suffer the constant possibility of displacement as these capital-intensive industries require less workers thus reducing job opportunities for women in general.

WOMEN IN THE SERVICE SECTOR

A feature in the structural transformation of any developing economy is the growth of the service sector. It is a common trend that the higher the level of economic development (as indicated by the Gross National Product), the greater is the size of the service sector. Such is the situation in developing Malaysia. The service sector is the most rapidly expanding sector in our economy, the most dynamic in its creation of new employment. Between 1957–1970 this sector showed an increase of 130.1%. In fact it has now succeeded the agricultural sector as the main employer of women labour. In 1957, 11.6% of women in the labour force were employed in the service sector, by 1980, it had increased to 36.4%. The service sector can be categorized into three main services, that is:

1. "Old" services: these consist of those activities which flourished before the period of rapid industrialization, for e.g. domestic services, housekeeping, etc.
2. "Complementary" services: these types of services have a direct correlation with the rise of manufacturing production, that is, they are complementary to the process of industrialization, for e.g. banking, finance, transportation, wholesale and retail trade.
3. "New" services: these include all those services that service the consumption of manufactured products, for e.g. education, consumption of modern clinical and medical services and entertainment.[28]

In 1957, 11.6% of the total female labour force were in the service sector and in terms of female employment, it was the second most important sector after agriculture. By 1970, the percentage had risen to 16.4%. In the earlier phase of Malaysia's economic development, that is, between the years 1957 and 1970, a significant part of the service sector expansion was occurring in the "old" services. These domestic-related services are compatible to the reproductive role of women and can be seen as an extension of women's activities at home. Thus, the majority of women worked as maids, house-keepers and cooks. But then in the following decade, the trend shifted towards an increase in the "new" and "complementary" services. This was in line with the new emergence of alternate employment within the service sector. In fact, women's participation in the commercial sector, a category of the "complementary" services, more than doubled. In 1970, their participation was at 5.2% but by 1980, it had increased to 12.7%. Within this period, the general increase in the percentage share of Malaysian women in the service sector was from 14.8% to 19.4%. By 1980, the most important sub-industries in the service sector were education, public administration and domestic.[29] Thus, it can be concluded that although women are still concentrated in domestic-related occupations yet the percentage share shows a decline in this type of occupation since more and more women are turning to other categories of employment within the service sector. Overall, the pattern of women's participation shows a direct correlation with structural changes in the economy.

The domestic service offers rural women, who are often unskilled, with job opportunities and the chance to move to the city. In a study conducted by the United Nations in Malaysia, it was found that most of those employed in the service sector are rural migrants.[30] The ready employment offered by the domestic service also serves as a "mid-way occupation" for most women before they find a more suitable or profitable job. It therefore facilitates a form of upward mobility in the urban areas. The increasing percentage of women in sectors such as banking, education and finance indicates this trend as well as the transformation in the occupational structure.

The service sector continues to possess a strong positive association with female employment and economic development. Yet most women are still at the lower rung of the occupational ladder. Even with economic development, the position of women as a whole in the service sector has not experienced much change. Their employment has improved quantitatively but not qualitatively.

CHARACTERISTICS OF WOMEN IN THE WORKFORCE

From available data, certain traits of women in the workforce can be identified, for instance:

1. The female workforce component in general is more elastic than the male, that is, women represent the "reserve army of labour" and thus are the most vulnerable to economic fluctuations. They are more prone to suffer the "last hired, first fired" syndrome as exemplified by cases in the manufacturing sector.
2. A 1979 report of the Labour Force Survey demonstrates that divorced women held the highest female LFPRs, that is, at 72%. This is followed by single women (55%), widowed women (46%) and married women (43%). This fact counters the "supplementary family wage" argument adopted by many employers in order to justify their practice of under-paying their women workers.
3. Malaysia's female labour force is comparatively young and thus very trainable. In 1980, out of the total female labour force of 1.7 million, 40% were under 25 years of age.
4. Most female workers bear the "double burden" of running a home whilst managing their career.

In view of the above, much can be done to improve women's lot in the labour force. The following section will provide some basic recommendations:

1. Reconceptualize "work" so that it will encompass the actual participation of women in all sectors of the economy, including unpaid labour in the domestic sphere.
2. Broader areas of education and training should be offered to young women, especially those in the technical, business and management fields. Gender-stereotyping, even as it exists in the education curriculum, should be minimized as far as possible.
3. Women's share in employment resources and sources of income should be protected through legislation, that is, the Government should institute joint property rights and equal accessibility to land ownership.
4. The Government and employers should set up day-care centres and well-equipped creche facilities in residential areas and work-sites to reduce the workload of women. Women should also be granted more flexible work-hours and leave.

5. Standard health and safety policies should be implemented more rigorously in all sectors, especially in the labour-intensive plantation and manufacturing sectors where work conditions are rather unfavourable.
6. Finally, the nation's development planners should include, as one of their goals, women's development and their economic self-sufficiency.

CONCLUSION

The evolution of Malaysian female labour force participation occurred in different phases following structural changes in the economy of the country.[33] The pattern of female employment here in Malaysia is similar to that of most developing countries. The restructuring due to economic development has brought about a major shift in labour from the primary–agricultural sector to the secondary–industrialized sector. This has caused the growing emergence of female labour in non-agricultural sectors. Sectors such as manufacturing and services have grown rapidly, absorbing an ever-increasing number of women workers.

The possibility of Malaysian women participating and succeeding in income-generating activities inherently depends on their ability to manage multiple roles. Though orthodox religious values and gender ideology and practices usually inhibit a woman's career mobility, the women of Malaysia generally do not encounter insurmountable socio-cultural problems. Basic gender discrimination certainly does exist in the workplace. Policy-wise there should be no discrepancy between male-female wages but it still exists in the private sector where some employers pay unequal wages and insist upon viewing a woman's salary as supplementary to a man's. But effective implementation of legislation and enforcement can overcome this. Women on the other hand should utilize the developing economic and socio-political situation to their own benefit. They should make full use of the new financial facilities and economic opportunities made available by structural adjustment measures whilst keeping abreast of and adapting to the changing economic situation. Only then can women hope to achieve greater economic autonomy and just rewards for their participation in the nation's development process.

NOTES

[1] As elaborated by Siti Rohani Yahya (1989), pp. 6–7. The general concept of workforce is the supply of labour and it is a simplistic concept: "people who are either at work or are seeking work." In Peninsular Malaysia, workforce or labour force refers to those who, during the reference week were in the 15–64 years age group (completed years at last birthday) and who were either employed or unemployed as defined below.

All persons who at any time during the reference week did any work for pay, profit or family gains (as an employer, own-account worker or unpaid family worker) are said to be *employed*. Persons who did not work during the reference week because of illness, injury, disability, bad weather, vacation, labour dispute and social or religious reasons but had a job, farm, enterprise or other family enterprise to return to are considered to be employed. These also include those on temporary layoff with pay who would definitely be called back to work. Employed persons at work and who had worked less than 30 hours during the reference week because of the nature of their work or due to insufficient work and were able and willing to accept additional hours of work were considered *underemployed*.

The unemployed includes both actively and inactively unemployed persons. *Actively unemployed* includes all persons who did not work during the reference week but were actively looking for work during the reference week. *Inactively unemployed* includes persons who were not looking for work because they believed no work was available, or if available they were not qualified, those who would have looked for work if they had not been temporarily ill or had it not been for bad weather, those who were waiting for answers to job applications and those who had looked for work prior to the reference week. On the other hand, all persons not classified as employed or unemployed as stated above, that is, housewives, students (including those going for further studies), retired or disabled persons and those not interested in looking for a job are considered to be *outside the labour force*.

Persons working without pay are excluded unless they meet certain stated conditions, that is, they are helpers in a family business or farm and they usually work thirty hours or more a

week. Persons doing only unpaid housework are especially excluded.
2. Amarjit Kaur, p. 2
3. Ibid., p. 4
4. Shamsulbahriah Ku Ahmad, p. 2
5. Lang Chin Ying, p. 8
6. Chia Seow Yue, p. 164
7. Ibid., p. 165
8. Ibid., p. 165
9. Siti Rohani Yahya, p. 16
10. Chia Seow Yue, p. 172
11. Siti Rohani Yahya, p. 14
12. Ibid., p. 21
13. Shamsulbahriah Ku Ahmad, p. 2
14. Chia Seow Yue, p. 178
15. Cecelia Ng, p. 14
16. Ibid., p. 18
17. Ibid., p. 11
18. Ibid., p. 11
19. Ibid., p. 16
20. Lang Chin Ying, p. 2
21. Ibid., p. 4
22. Ibid., p. 11
23. Ibid., p. 7
24. Ibid., p. 12
25. Jamilah Ariffin, p. 8
26. Ibid., p. 8
27. Jamilah Ariffin, pp. 12,15
28. Faridah Shahadan and Madeline Berma, pp. 25–26
29. Ibid., p. 21
30. Ibid., p. 27
31. Ibid., p. 27
32. Chia Seow Yue, p. 175
33. Faridah Shahadan and Madeline Berma, p. 3

BIBLIOGRAPHY

Annuar Ali, "Industrial Restructuring: Beyond the Industrial Master Plan." Paper presented at the *MIER 1988 National Outlook Conference, November, 1988.*

Chia, Siow Yue, "Women's economic participation in Malaysia", adapted from *Women's Economic Participation in Asia and the Pacific*, U.N., Economic and Social Commission for Asia and The Pacific, 1987.

Faridah Shahadan and Berma, Madeline, "Economic Development Trends and Women's Participation in the Service Sector: A macro-level analysis of interrelationships, impact and implication on development planning, 1957–1980." Paper presented at the Colloquium on "Women and Development—Implications for Planning and Population Dynamics", University of Malaya, January 1989.

Jamilah Ariffin, "Economic Development and Women in the Manufacturing Sector—A macro-level analysis and with reference to 'Women and Development' issues." Paper presented at the Colloquium on "Women and Development in Malaysia—Implications for Planning and Population Dynamics", January 1989.

Jamilah Ariffin (1980), "The Position of Women Workers in the Manufacturing Industries in Malaysia" in Evelyn Hong, *Malaysian Women: Problems and Issues*, CAP Publications, Penang.

Jamilah Ariffin (1984), "Impact of Modern Electronics Technology on Women Workers in Malaysia" in Aziz, Yip and Ling (eds.), *Technology, Culture and Development*, University of Malaya Press, 1984.

Jamilah Ariffin (1982), "Industrialization, Female Labour Migration and Changing Pattern of Malay Women's Labour Force Participation" in *Journal of South-East Asian Studies.*"

Kamal Salih, "The Changing Face of the Malaysian Economy", *Seminar on Business Opportunities and Entrepreneurship*, Kuala Lumpur, 1987.

Kaur, Amarjit, "An Historical Analysis of Women's Economic Participation in Development." Paper presented at the Colloquium on "Women and Development—Implications for Planning and Population Dynamics", University of Malaya, January 1989.

Lang, Chin Ying, "Women in Business." Paper presented at the Colloquium on "Women and Development—Implications for Planning and Population Dynamics", University of Malaya, January 1989.

Ng, Cecelia, "Impact of Agricultural Development on Rural Women: From Producer to Housewife?". Paper presented at the Colloquium on "Women and Development—Implications for Planning and Population Dynamics", University of Malaya, January 1989.

Shamsulbahriah Ku Ahmad, "Stratification and Occupational Segmentation in the Peninsular Malaysian Labour Force: A case for gender-oriented development planning." Paper presented at the Colloquium on "Women and Development—Implications for Planning and Population Dynamics", University of Malaya, January 1989.

Siti Rohani Yahya, "The Development Process and Women's Labour Force Participation—A macro-level analysis of patterns and trends, 1957–1987." Paper presented at the Colloquium on "Women and Development—Implications for Planning and Population Dynamics", University of Malaya, January 1989.

3
Women's Participation In Education In Malaysia

Education is the act or process of acquiring knowledge. In more ways than one, it is also a means for the development of character and mental powers. The value of education is unquestionable. Many people in Malaysia have achieved economic mobility and enhanced their status through education. Therefore, education not only enables a person to develop his mental faculties but also helps him progress in his social environment.

It has been argued by several researchers, for example, O'Brien (1959), that the main means of recruitment into the modern occupational labour force is by way of education and subsequent certification. In societies based on the capitalist mode of production, education is a commodity—a marketable skill. Those with the more socially valued types of education and those with the most education generally have better occupational opportunities than those without it.[1] This statement itself points to the importance of education.

Basically, in developing countries such as Malaysia, tertiary or university education serves as the ultimate dream for a person wishing to gain social recognition. Unfortunately, in the past, women were given limited access to formal education as compared to men. At present, this is still somewhat true in the case of higher education. Some people with strict traditional beliefs are generally still biased against granting women the opportunity to acquire the highest level of education and equal access to all fields of study. In the recent past, studies in the field of Arts were considered more appropriate for women rather than in the field of Science.

Malaysia, being a nation with a multi-racial population, has varied and distinct religious, social and cultural beliefs, values and norms. However, until the 1960s, there was a common traditional belief that women are ideally better off as housewives, and when educated, should be channelled into teaching, nursing and other such "feminine" occupations.

The aim of this chapter is to provide an overview of women's participation in education in Malaysia for the period 1957 to 1987. The discussion will include both formal and non-formal education.

HISTORICAL BACKGROUND OF WOMEN'S EDUCATION DURING THE COLONIAL PERIOD

British colonial rule had undeniably developed the formal education system in Malaya. It has also influenced post-colonial education policies and systems. Under the "Divide and Rule" policy, the British created separate educational structures and distributed the educational facilities unevenly according to ethnicity and geographical location. This caused the discrepancies among the individual education systems of the different ethnic groups. Each ethnic group also had different and unique reactions toward the colonial education system during that period. For example, the Malays were generally prejudiced against the colonial English education because they were convinced that formal westernized education would cause disorderliness and irreligiousness among their Moslem children. There was the fear that the children would be influenced by Christianity in the English missionary schools. Conversely, the Chinese, as a migrant stock, saw a good future in English education. They were keen to send their children to English schools and were partly responsible for financing some of their own major educational institutions. Schools were also provided for the Indian children of estate workers. Many of the Indian parents were optimistic about English education and encouraged their children to study in English schools. Better schools were located in the urban areas than in rural areas thus generating unequal access to good education.

Under those prevailing conditions, women in Malaysia at that period of time who came from deprived economic groups, such as the poor estate plantation families and peasant families with minimal resources, tended to be educationally disadvantaged and deprived.

In addition, the traditional belief that girls should stay at home provided the main objection to girls being educated. Daughters were not only discouraged from going out for fear of society's censure; they were made to believe that the place of a woman is in the kitchen. In conforming to society's traditional norms, parents played a big part in encouraging and perpetuating this view. They were also responsible for their daughters' lack of interest in education for the parents only provided their sons with opportunities, motivation and encouragement to pursue a formal education. Traditional families believed that daughters had no reason to go to school because, ultimately, they would all be married off and become housewives. As O'Brien puts it, " the patriarchal belief [was] that a woman does not *need* a career because she is always someone's daughter, later someone's wife".[2]

In traditional social structures, interaction between boys and girls was disapproved, thus there was a need to establish separate schools for them. As can be expected, there were more boys' schools than girls' schools. In 1938, there was a total of 29 English medium girls' schools compared to 76 boys' schools. Clearly, more schools were established for boys during this period. This formed a very strong foundation for emphasizing and favouring education for males over females and the basis for unequal educational opportunities between the sexes.

PART I
FORMAL EDUCATION

Early Education For Women, 1938–1967

Despite the obstacles to women's participation in education as discussed above, more girls were attending school during this period. Both the Malay-medium and English-medium schools showed an increase in female participation from 1938 to 1967. As expected, due to Malay prejudices against education for girls, the Malay-medium schools started with a lower percentage of girls attending schools, that is, 28.6% compared to the English-medium schools, that is, 32.4% in 1938. (See Table 3.1). In 1947, Malay-medium schools had an enrolment of 28.2% while the English-medium schools had a percentage of 34.9%. However, by 1957, with growing political awareness, Malay parents wanted formal education for their daughters. Hence, Malay-medium schools showed a fantastic increase in enrolment, that is, to 42.6% as compared to the English-medium schools which increased only by 4.1% to 38.8%. Ten years later, the percentage of girls attending Malay-medium schools was 49.6%. This figure was far above that of the English-medium schools which stood at 41.0%.

By the pre-Second World War period, existing attitudes against women's participation in education were losing ground. In the secondary schools, the percentage of girls attending the English and Malay-medium schools charted a general increase.(See figures in Table 3.2). Statistics are not available for the Malay-medium secondary schools but the English-medium secondary schools in 1938 registered a female enrolment of 27.1%. In the post-war period, as in 1957, this increased to 35.4%. In the very same year, the percentage of girls attending Malay-medium schools was 27.7%. Although the female enrolment in Malay-medium schools was relatively much lower than the English-medium schools in 1947, this changed considerably ten years later. The female enrolment percentages of both schools were almost on par, that is, 40.3% and 40.1% respectively.

It is interesting to note that from the year 1957, which marked the year of Malaya's political independence, the number of girls attending both primary and secondary schools increased greatly. For example, the percentage of girls attending primary Malay-medium schools in 1947 was 28.3%. This increased to 42.6% in 1957 and reached 49.6% in 1967. Similarly, a significant increase was apparent for the English-medium schools. For example, in 1947, the percentage of girls attending secondary schools was 25.7%, and this advanced to 35.4% in 1957. This figure made an enormous leap to 40.1% a decade later, in 1967. This trend can be explained because, generally, formal education in the form of schooling was made more accessible to all individuals after Independence. The Malaysian people were also more aware of the importance of formal education as a means to better employment opportunities and hence, a better standard of life.

It was therefore surprising that women's participation at the tertiary level during this period was low. For instance, University Malaya, the only university in the country at that time, had an overall female student enrolment of 19.8% in 1959. This figure increased to 25.9% in 1964 and finally attained a percentage of 28.7% at the end of the Sixties.

Table 3.1
Enrolment By Sex And Medium In Assisted Primary Schools From Standards One To Six, 1938–1967

Medium	Sex	1938	1947	1957	1967
Malay	Total	56,904	164,528	441,567	591,560
	Boys	40,613	118,043	253,450	299,051
	Girls	16,291	46,485	168,117	293,509
English	Total	32,141	45,174	130,360	289,056
	Boys	21,742	29,418	79,713	170,517
	Girls	10,399	15,756	50,647	118,539
Chinese	Total	47,411	139,191	310,458	355,771
	Boys	33,656	99,306	186,677	187,128
	Girls	13,755	39,885	123,781	168,643
Tamil	Total	22,820	33,954	50,766	79,203
	Boys	15,584	20,834	26,153	38,033
	Girls	7,236	13,120	24,613	41,170

Source: Completed from Educational Statistics, 1938–1967, Ministry of Education, Malaysia. Please note that the statistics for the year 1938 are for the Straits Settlements and Federated Malay States only. Those for the period 1947 to 1967 are for Peninsular Malaysia.

Table 3.2
Enrolment By Sex And Medium In Assisted Secondary Schools From Remove To Upper Six, 1938–1967

Medium	Sex	1938	1947	1957	1967
Malay	Total	Not available	Not available	2,315	128,069
	Boys			1,674	76,454
	Girls			641	51,615
English	Total	17,353	12,510	48,235	286,254
	Boys	12,651	9,298	31,180	171,537
	Girls	4,702	3,212	17,055	114,717
Chinese	Total	3,215	2,692	30,052	Not available
	Boys	2,149	1,953	20,806	
	Girls	1,066	739	9,246	
Tamil	Total	15	93	440	Not available
	Boys	9	84	314	
	Girls	6	9	126	

Source: Compiled from Educational Statistics of Malaysia, 1938–1967, Ministry of Education, Malaysia.

The following data illustrate the unequal position of female students in the university and technical colleges, especially in the sciences. The Engineering course, being male-dominated had no female students from 1959 until 1963. In 1964, records show that there was a female undergraduate student, but curiously enough, there is no record of her graduating. Thus, the assumption is that she must have dropped out. In 1970, there were only two female Engineering students as compared to 390 male students. A similar pattern was found in the Agriculture course. In 1960, there were only two females from the total of 27 students. This amounted to 7.4% which subsequently decreased to 6.6% in 1969, that is, there were eighteen females out of 274 students. The medical course, which was relatively a new field, was first introduced in 1963 and there were five female students who formed 17.1% of all the students in the Medical Faculty. Females who enrolled at the College of Agriculture in 1959 for the first time represented 4% of the total student population. This figure decreased in the early Sixties and by 1964, only 3.5% of female students were recorded. However, in 1969, there was an increase to 13.4%, that is, 76 females out of 565 students. At the Technical College, the enrolment of females kept on increasing from a sole female in 1957 to 28 in 1964. By the end of the Sixties, the female percentage at the college reached 7.5%.

Thus, in terms of early education, from primary to tertiary levels, the participation rate of females was inadequate. With such a poor beginning, it is not surprising that women in Malaysia faced a tough challenge in attaining equal levels of education with the men.

Education For Women In The 1970s

In the 1970s, in Peninsular Malaysia, female enrolment in schools continued to increase.[3] In 1970, when compared to male enrolment at the primary level for the age-group 6+ to 11+ which was recorded at 91.6%, female enrolment was outstanding at 84.8%. On the whole, females constituted 47.3% of the total enrolment at the primary level of education. The percentage of females of the primary schools' student population rose persistently and by 1979, the female enrolment reached a percentage of 48.7%.

However, female enrolment at the secondary level was not very encouraging. In 1970, only 43.6% of the female population between the age-group of 12+ to 14+ was registered in the lower-secondary level. In comparison, the male population of that age-group had a lower-secondary level enrolment of 60.6%. The females at this level made up 41.1% of the total student enrolment. By 1979, it had risen to 47.7%.

At the upper-secondary level, female participation was even more dismal. In 1970, only 16.1% of the female population in the school-going age-group of 15+ to 16+ were attending the upper-secondary schools. The female students made up 39.5% of the total student enrolment at this level. In 1975, this figure increased to 42.6%. However, developments after 1975 to 1979 could not be traced because statistics for this period were not available.

Female enrolment rates at the post-secondary level was really meagre, that is, only 2.2% of the female population in the school-going age-group of 17+ to 19+ were receiving post-secondary education. On the other hand, the rate of males of this age-group attending post-secondary level schools was almost double, that is, 4.1%. In general, the females constituted 33.8% of the total student population at the post-secondary level. By the end of the 1970s, the female enrolment at this level increased to 44.6%.

The 1970s showed a relatively poor participation of female students at university level. Female students comprised only 0.4% of the population who were qualified to be at university. The percentage for the males was twice that of the females', that is, 0.8%. In the three universities and two colleges of that time, female students formed 29.1% of total student enrolment. In 1979, 33.9% of the total student population in the five universities comprised females. During the 1970s, females who were attending university were mainly concentrated in the Arts field. At the University of Malaya, for example, 39.1% of students in the Arts Faculty were females as compared to 8.6% in the Agriculture Faculty.

In the Engineering Faculty, the number of females was even more insignificant, that is, only 0.6% were females. Females at the Universiti Kebangsaan Malaysia (UKM) were also concentrated in the Arts Faculty. In 1972, 29.5% of total students in the Arts Faculty comprised females as compared to 10.8% in the Science Faculty. However, by 1979, a change was evident. The Science Faculty had a female enrolment of 30.9% and the Medical Faculty had an equally satisfying female enrolment, that is, 31.1%.

It can be summarized that the general pattern of female participation in higher education reflects a consequential development of their low participation rates at primary school level.

Women's Participation In Education In The 1980s

Female participation rates in the 1980s reflect a continuation of the changing trend that had risen in the 1970s. In 1983, females formed 48.5% of the primary school populace throughout Malaysia. This figure rose to 48.6% in 1986 and remained at that percentage in 1987 and then moved upwards to 48.9% in 1988.[4]

Female participation in the lower-secondary schools is equally encouraging. In 1983, females constituted 48.4% of the total student population, and this figure rose to 48.8% in 1986. In 1987, it rose to 49.1% and subsequently to 49.6% in 1988.

Similarly, female enrolment in the upper secondary schools has also advanced considerably, as compared to the previous decade. Females constituted 48.8% of the total student population in 1983, rising to 49.2% in 1986 and 50.2% in 1987 and eventually reaching 51.2% in 1988. It is apparent therefore that in the 1980s, as far as the formal "general" education schools are concerned, females have finally attained an equal position with males. However, in the technical secondary schools, enrolment is still very much male-dominated. Only 35% of the Form 4 students and 34.7% of Form 5 students in these schools were female. The vocational schools also showed a similar trend. The Form 4 female student enrolment stood at 22.6% and for Form 5, it was 24.5%. Vocational education is still gender-specific and male-dominated. Most of the females who are in vocational training are concentrated in service-oriented fields such as hotel-catering, preparation of food, beauty-care, tailoring, etc. On the other hand, the male students are mainly in fields like building and woodwork.[5] Basically, the main portion of female students is found in the academic and "feminine" fields.

It is interesting to note that the situation cited above does not occur for post-secondary schools with a non-technical curriculum. Female enrolment at the post-secondary level was 50.1% of the total enrolment in 1983. In 1986, it decreased slightly to 49.2% but the following year showed an increase, that is, to 54.3%. In 1988, it attained a percentage of 54.4%.

At the university level, in the 1980s, there seemed to be a marked increase in female enrolment. In 1983, the total female enrolment was 38.8% in the six universities (including the International Islamic University). Three years later, there was a total of seven universities with the establishment of the Universiti Utara Malaysia (UUM). The overall enrolment of female students was 40.8% in 1986 and 41.2% in 1987.

It is, however, obvious from the Government statistics that females were still taking up studies in the Arts or teaching fields. They tended to steer away from Agriculture and Engineering courses. The Arts Faculty in 1985 had a total female enrolment of 975 female students which formed 53.2% of total student population while the Engineering Faculty had a low female enrolment, that is, 14.5%. However, in the 1980s, it is evident there has been a slight shift from the usual concentration of male students in courses such as Business, Science and Medicine. For example, in 1985, at the Universiti Kebangsaan Malaysia (UKM), there were 376 females or 42.3% studying Business Management, 427 females or 51.8% were reading Medicine and 703 females or 56.0% female students in the Science Faculty.

At the Universiti Sains Malaysia (USM) too, females formed only 21.9% of the total enrolment in the Building and Planning Faculty and 22.9% in the Applied Sciences Faculty in 1985. Female enrolment in the Engineering and Industrial Technology Faculty was only 25.4%. In the Science Faculty, women made up more than half of the student population but this was because they monopolized the course termed "Science with Education". Similarly, they constituted more than half of the total population in the Humanities with Education and Mass Communication faculties, that is, 71.4% and 58.2% respectively.

A similar trend is observed at the University of Malaya (UM)— the females dominate the Science with Education course. As expected, their participation is rather lacking in the Engineering Faculty. At the Universiti Pertanian Malaysia (UPM), their participation rates are equally low in the Engineering and Agriculture courses. In Universiti Teknologi Malaysia (UTM), in 1985, there were no females registered in studies related to Petroleum Engineering, Marine Engineering and Aeronautical Engineering.

Effects Of Formal Education:
Educational Attainment And Literacy

Educational attainment means more than just the development of mental skills. It is only natural to expect substantial changes to take place in the home, work and social environment when women have received higher education and attained educational qualifications.

To begin with, when women start going to school, they leave domestic seclusion. In the process of educating themselves, women realize that their place is not, as traditional beliefs and norms dictate, only at home. Socially, society has to start adjusting to the new generation of working women who have attained higher education. This will bring about changes at the workplace where male workers have to put up with competition from their female colleagues. With the acquisition of higher education and training, women are more equipped to face society intellectually.

Aside from that, changes are apparent in the personal aspect. Through education, women manage to cultivate a better self-image and greater self-confidence which eventually encourage them to have independent values and aspirations. This would indirectly mean a change in the social scene where women will be inclined to fight for their rights.

All these changes are bound to occur as long as women continue to attain higher education and procure paid occupations. It has been pointed out that, in the 1970s, the educational attainment among females was still lower than the males, 61.4% for females as compared to 84.6% for males. (See Table 3.3). But in 1980, there was an increase in the female percentage, that is, 71.9%, but the male percentage was still higher at 85.4%. However, on the whole, the rate of increase is higher for females than males although the level of educational attainment for the males is still higher. This is probably due to the increased opportunities for females to acquire formal education. From 1970 to 1980, an increase was shown in the number of females who attained formal education as far as Form One, Form Two, and also at the School Certificate and Higher School Certificate levels.

Greater educational participation rates for females were also reflected in their literacy rates. For example, in 1970, the literacy level for females was 47%. (See Table 3.4). This figure increased to 64% in 1980. For the males, the literacy level in 1970 was 69% and in 1980, it was 80%. The literacy level among females for both years proved to be lower than the males but the increase in literacy rate from 1970 to 1980 was higher for the females than the males, that is, 17% and 11% respectively. This is indicative of the fact that although the male literacy level is higher than the female, there is a tendency for more females to become literate at a greater rate than males.

Table 3.3
Percentage Distribution Of Population
By Educational Attainment And Sex In Malaysia For 1970 And 1980

Educational Attainment	1970 Male No.	1970 Male %	1970 Female No.	1970 Female %	1970 Total No.	1970 Total %	1980 Male No.	1980 Male %	1980 Female No.	1980 Female %	1980 Total No.	1980 Total %
At least some education (7 years +)	3,267,660	84.6	2,452,401	61.4	5,720,061	71.3	4,490,518	85.4	3,820,466	71.9	8,310,984	78.6
At least Form 1 (13 years +)	861,676	27.8	527,363	16.9	1,389,039	22.4	1,889,803	44.8	1,477,068	34.2	3,366,871	39.5
At least Form 2 (15 years +)	573,015	20.2	336,332	11.8	931,807	16.4	1,409,244	36.3	1,090,116	27.3	2,499,360	30.0
At least School Certificate (37 years +)	184,959	7.1	96,217	3.7	281,176	5.4	697,930	20.0	402,396	10.9	1,100,326	13.1
At least HSC with Certificate (18 years +)	29,814	1.2	10,564	0.4	40,678	0.8	152,756	4.5	77,800	2.2	230,556	3.3

"Years +" refers to those with education exceeding the number of years stated but not attaining that of the following category of the table.

Source: The figures for 1970 were culled from Table 4.6, 1979, General Report Population Census of Malaysia, Volume 1, while the 1980 figures were calculated from the 1980 Census of Malaysia.

Table 3.4
Literacy Rate In Malaysia—1979 And 1980

Age-Group And Sex	1970 Number (Thousand)	1970 Literate	1970 Semiliterate (Percentage)	1970 Illiterate	1980 Number (Thousand)	1980 Literate	1980 Semiliterate (Percentage)	1980 Illiterate
10—14								
Male	703.5	70	7	23	829.9	85	4	10
Female	682.5	66	6	27	800.6	85	4	11
Total	1,396.0	68	7	25	1,630.5	85	4	11
15—19								
Male	555.5	84	3	12	731.0	91	2	7
Female	569.5	75	4	22	753.6	88	2	10
Total	1,125.0	80	4	17	1,484.6	90	2	9
20—29								
Male	742.5	81	4	15	1,106.2	89	2	9
Female	764.5	60	4	35	1,192.0	80	3	17
Total	1,507.0	71	4	25	2,298.2	85	2	13
30—39								
Male	554.8	69	5	26	774.2	84	3	13
Female	570.2	34	5	62	760.7	62	4	34
Total	1,125.0	51	5	44	1,534.9	73	4	24

Table 3.4—Continued
Literacy Rate In Malaysia—1970 And 1980

40—49							
Male	401.4	60	5	35	546.2	72	4	24
Female	403.2	20	4	76	544.3	35	5	60
Total	804.6	40	4	56	1,090.6	54	4	42
50—59							
Male	300.4	51	5	44	362.2	62	4	34
Female	279.7	10	3	87	368.8	21	4	75
Total	580.0	31	4	65	731.0	41	4	54
60—69							
Male	280.5	35	5	60	365.7	43	5	51
Female	258.9	4	2	94	376.1	9	3	88
Total	539.3	20	4	76	741.9	26	4	70
10 and over							
Male	3,538.7	69	5	26	4,715.5	80	3	16
Female	3,528.4	47	4	49	4,796.2	64	3	33
Total	7,067.0	58	5	38	9,511.7	72	3	25

Source: Jomo Kwame Sundaram and Tan Peck Leng, Not The Better Half: Malaysian Women in Development Planning, 1984.

PART II
NON-FORMAL EDUCATION FOR WOMEN

As has been elaborated in the first part of this chapter, the formal education system has been the main avenue for women's participation in education in Malaysia. However, the Government has also pursued plans and programmes for women's participation in non-formal education. This part of the paper shall discuss the programmes of non-formal education affecting women. Unfortunately, the scope of the discussion is limited as available statistics on women's participation in non-formal education is not adequate for a detailed discussion.

Non-formal education is organized by a variety of bodies, for example, Government departments and agencies, the police and armed forces, private organizations and industries, voluntary associations, labour unions, political parties and individuals.[6]

Like formal education, non-formal learning serves the same purpose of educating women intellectually and preparing them to seek employment outside the home. There are various adult-education programmes, for example, further education classes and private education courses. "Further education" classes, which started in 1958, is a programme where education is made accessible to those who are not able to get proper education, either due to advanced age or prior commitments to their jobs. With further education classes they are able to continue their education and improve their qualifications. Moreover, further education classes now also cater for private schools and non-formal school candidates who wish to sit for normal-school exams.

Also, aside from the formal adult-education courses that are run by the Government, there are also private schools that conduct tailoring, secretarial, modelling and hair-dressing classes specifically for women. Although there are no available statistical data on the number and range of these private institutions, their contribution to income-generating skills for women cannot be underestimated.[7]

The Ministry of Labour and Manpower, the Ministry of Culture, Youth and Sports, the Ministry of Agriculture and MARA all play a major part in the non-formal education programmes. These bodies are responsible for the short courses and on-the-job training schemes which help to cultivate a youth's vocational, technical and industrial skills. Female youths are specially trained in courses such as tailoring, hair-dressing and home science.

The process of educating poor women is also not neglected. Two specific examples of pioneer income-generating projects organized for this purpose were the ASEAN-Australia Project and Sang Kancil Project. Both projects which started in 1979 were aimed to involve women in national development and improve their socio-economic status, especially women in the rural areas. The ASEAN-Australia project was under the ASEAN Population Programme and was financed by the Australian Government and coordinated by the ASEAN Population Coordination Unit. Under such a scheme, poor rural women were encouraged to learn skills in food and handicraft production, tailoring and rental of crockery. Vocational training was also provided. Eventually, participants of this project started child-minding centres, tuition classes for school-children and vocational classes. The Sang Kancil project is similar to that of the ASEAN-Australia Project. Sang Kancil centres were set up in urban slums where activities dealing with handicrafts, ceramic-ware production and book-binding were undertaken by poor women. The women were also educated on matters dealing with bulk-selling, cooperatives and leadership.

Part of the non-formal education programmes also include adult education and community development classes. These classes are organized particularly for the rural peasant women in accordance with the national rural development programme. Originally, the adult education classes were aimed at abolishing illiteracy amongst the adult population and simultaneously increasing their participation in development programmes. Subsequently, the programmes expanded to include other community-oriented activities. The division leading this project is called Community Development Division of the Ministry of National and Rural Development or KEMAS, its acronym in the national language. This division arranges classes which generate income-generating skills for rural people. However, again the male-female dichotomy is apparent. The male participants involved in this project are more inclined to be equipped for vocational work such as motor-mechanics, carpentry, radio-repair, arts and craft while domestic science classes like cooking, personal care and hygiene, needlework and general home economics classes are made available to the women participants. These women participants are expected to contribute to national development primarily through their domestic role in the family and secondarily, through their work participation in the economy.

As mentioned earlier, this programme is part of an overall plan to develop the poor rural women. In this process of re-educating the rural women, three agencies are responsible, that is, KEMAS, FELDA (specifically the Settler Development Division of the Federal Land Development Authority) and RISDA (Rubber Smallholders Development Authority). They provide home-economics, child-care development and leadership courses. For example, the courses set up by KEMAS are aimed at complementing rural development programmes in some of the rural villages. The courses conducted by the Settler Development Division of FELDA, on the other hand, attempt to improve the living standards of the settler population. In fact, non-formal education of the women settlers is part of a scheme to activate them into participating in the rural development programme.

CONCLUSION

Women's participation rates in education, whether formal or non-formal, appear to be increasing; rising firstly in the 1970s and maintaining a steady increase in the 1980s.

Overtly, there seems to be no sex discrimination in Malaysian society but in reality, this is not so. There are still certain fields of education and employment that women would not be encouraged to venture into. Women are deemed by conservative elements in society as not capable of handling the "masculine" fields of employment relating to Engineering and Agriculture Sciences as they demand much heavier work outside the home. There is also a persistent view that women's primary role is to take care of the home and therefore working women will not be able to effectively combine their roles as good mothers and efficient workers. Therefore, teaching in schools which is "half-day" work is still considered by many people as the best job for working married women as they will be able to fulfill their traditional role as nurturing mothers and good housewives.

There is a need to overcome these prejudices as well as to provide state and national level child-care support system so as to ease the dual burden responsibilities of working mothers. Women should be given equal opportunity and encouragement to pursue education in all fields which they desire. Perhaps in the near future, more people, women as well as men, will come out to claim for equal access to all forms of education for women, especially in the fields where women are not so well represented. For example, if women are given greater encouragement and opportunities to attend the technical courses at school level, they will then gain easier and greater entrance to these courses at the tertiary level.

On the whole, Malaysian women's participation in education is improving and there are numerous signs of potential growth. With proper guidance from an enlightened Government and changing values in society, all women in Malaysia, regardless of race and class, should be given the opportunity to progress steadily in the field of education and to achieve gender equality.

NOTES

[1] O'Brien, Leslie, "Class, Sex and Ethnic Stratification in West Malaysia, with particular reference to women in the profession" (1979), p. 86

[2] O'Brien, Leslie, "Four paces behind: Women's work in Peninsular Malaysia", from *Women's work and Women's role*, ed. by Lenore Manderson (1983), p. 210

[3] Kaur, Manjit, "Women and Education: The Development of Women in Education in Malaysia and Some Implications for Planning and Population Dynamics" (1989). Percentages have been calculated by the writer based on absolute figures given in the Educational Statistics publications, p. 5

[4] Kaur, Manjit (1989), p. 7. Source of educational statistics for the years 1987 and 1988 from Unit Data, Bahagian Perancangan dan Penyelidikan Pendidikan, Ministry of Education, Malaysia.

[5] Nik Safiah Karim, "Wanita Malaysia sebelum dan sesudah dekad wanita" (1985), p. 7

[6] Jamilah Ariffin, "Aims and Methods of Lifelong Learning (or Re-education) in the Context of Women's Participation in Society and Lifelong Education" (1984), p. 12

[7] Jamilah Ariffin (1984), p. 13

BIBLIOGRAPHY

Byrne, Eileen M., *Women and Education*. Tavistock Publications Ltd., Great Britain, 1978.

Jamilah Ariffin, "The Aims and Methods of Lifelong Learning (or Re-education) in the Context of Women's Participation in

Society and Lifelong Education". Unpublished paper presented at the International Conference on "Women and Development", Saitama, Japan, October 1984.

Jayaweera, Swarna, "Class and Gender in Education and Employment". Unpublished paper, Colombo, December 1987.

Nik Safiah Karim, "Wanita Malaysia sebelum dan sesudah dekad wanita". Unpublished paper presented at the seminar "The Period of Women's Achievements and Challenges", Kuala Lumpur, August 1985.

Kaur, Manjit, "Women and Education: The development of women in education in Malaysia and some implications for planning and population dynamics". Paper presented at the Colloquium on "Women and Development in Malaysia—Implications for Planning and Population Dynamics", Population Studies Conference, University Malaya, January 1989.

Manderson, Lenore (ed.), *Women's work and Women's role*, The Australian National University, Australia, 1983.

O'Brien, Leslie, "Class, Sex and Ethnic Stratification in West Malaysia, with particular reference to women in the profession", Ph.D. Thesis, Monash University, Australia, 1979.

4

Women In Medicine And Other Health-Related Aspects

Health care is of central concern to women. The work women do within the home and outside, their role in the family, and the bearing and rearing of children, not only affect their health but in turn are also affected by it. Women require constant medical services because of their reproductive functions and therefore are in need of specific curative and preventive care. Secondly, women as mothers and homemakers are responsible for the overall standard of their families' health. The biological and social realities of their maternal role are therefore closely linked to their health status and are a major determinant of the problems they face in health, employment, education and in many other areas.

Therefore, the aim of this chapter is three-fold:

1. To discuss women's status and position with reference to mortality and fertility trends in Malaysia. This is evaluated within the context of their important role and function as reproducers of children, homemakers and contributors to the nation's economic progress.
2. To evaluate Malaysian women's access to health care facilities. Here, we will give an overview of the health facilities and maternal health services provided by the Government and private sector for women in the country. We will also look into the consequences of health services and facilities on the mortality and fertility trends of both men and women.

3. To discuss the reasons for and implications of Malaysian women's low participation in medicine. Although women usually prefer specific medical services from female obstetricians and gynaecologists, there are still very few women in this field of medicine.

Therefore, this chapter is divided into three parts according to the three major aims outlined above.

WOMEN'S HEALTH STATUS AND POSITION: A LOOK INTO MORTALITY AND FERTILITY TRENDS

Women's Status In Society And Its Effect On Their Health Care System

Normally, women's health status in a country is closely affected by their socio-economic role, class position and status in their society. When women have a subordinate position *vis-à-vis* men in society, complaints such as menstruation, pregnancy, childbirth, breast-feeding, menopause, are dismissed as "women's sickness" and are not given serious consideration which they deserve. Doctors and medical professionals produced in a male-oriented society immediately tend to connect all women's complaints to their reproductive system and their inferior physical strength.

According to the image perpetuated by unequal societies, such as the Victorian society of nineteenth-century England, the ideal woman is supposed to be weak and delicate but paradoxically should be able to perform all the domestic tasks necessary for the sustenance of the family. In almost all countries of the world it is the women who bear the major responsibility of house-keeping and the upbringing of children. For most women, especially the poorer ones, this means a double or triple workload when coupled with outside employment. This can only have a long-term detrimental effect on women's health as they become more prone to fatigue, mental and physical stress and this increases their susceptibility to illnesses. Regardless of their socio-economic status, women all over the world face very similar problems—everywhere they are often subject to laws, customs and mental attitudes which institutionalize their supposed physical inferiority and social subordination to men. As citizens with lesser education and employment opportunities, they are usually segregated into lower-paid arduous jobs such as working in an assembly line in electronics factories, as check-out counter clerks in big supermarkets, domestic workers and waitresses. Overwork, stress and strain, sexual harassment, hazards at the workplace and violence, all these adversely affect women's health.

Women also have to be particularly cautious of adverse physical health conditions because of their childbearing and delivery functions. Pregnancy, childbirth and breast-feeding drain a woman's health. But because of cultural influences, the majority of women, especially those belonging to the lower socio-economic status, are often undernourished. Within households, where women have a subordinate status, food is distributed in accordance with the status and position of an individual instead of the individual's nutritional requirements. In such circumstances, women and female children usually receive what is left over from the men's consumption of the daily meals. This is very bad for a childbearing woman because an undernourished mother tends to give birth to a small, underweight child who suffers three to four times the risk of dying, as compared to a better birth-weight baby.

As working women, housewives and mothers, the female human species are and have always been consumers and providers of health care, yet in most countries they generally have little or no control over the shaping of health services, research, the environment or the work they do. Whether it is forced sterilization as in Puerto Rico or the denial of sterilization to women who want it, as in France, or the increasing restrictions on abortion as in the United States, the result is the same—women do not usually have the right or sufficient power and authority at the national-level to control the health policies which affect their own bodies. This is indirectly a significant reflection of the State's perception about its women and women's designated role and status. It is also an accurate indicator of the *actual power status* of womenfolk in that society. On the other hand, mortality and fertility trends which are often utilized to portray the position of women actually reflects more accurately the *socio-economic and health status* of various categories of people—including women—in a given population. It is to these details that we now turn.

Mortality Trends

Since the late 1920s, Peninsular Malaysia has been experiencing mortality decline. Both the male and female categories of all the ethnic groups have recorded increased life expectancy, as shown in Figures 4.1 and 4.2. However, discrepancy exists among the various ethnic groups of the population despite the notable drop in the country's overall mortality rates. This section of the chapter will give special attention to the differences in the mortality trends of both the male and female in the various ethnic groups and also among the children.

Mortality Rates By Sex and Ethnic Groups

Before Independence in 1957, various tropical diseases such as malaria, beri-beri, small-pox, cholera, plague and rabies were responsible for the high record of mortality rates among the immigrant Indian and Chinese labourers.[1] However, due to the expansion of health services in the estates and towns, most of these diseases were wiped out. The Malays, on the other hand, were not greatly affected by these diseases, nor did they benefit from the improvement of health services at that time.[2]

As in Peninsular Malaysia, mortality rates in Sabah and Sarawak recorded a decline with the advent of better medical and health facilities. The Second World War and the Japanese Occupation caused a temporary disruption in the provision of medical facilities and services.[3]

The post-war period led to greater efforts towards improving the living standards of the different ethnic groups. Decline in mortality was apparent in the ages 0–5 years for both sexes and for females in the reproductive ages in the ethnic groups.[4] Figures 4.3 and 4.4 show the age-specific death rates by ethnic group and sex for the period 1984–1986. It is obvious that mortality rates are higher at younger and older ages. At both these extremes, the Chinese show lower mortality rates than the Malays and Indians. The mortality rates among Indian males of 35 years and above appear to be the highest among the three ethnic groups.

An analysis of the sex differentials of age-specific mortality rates reveals that before 1970, mortality rates were much higher among the females compared to the males, especially females in the childbearing ages of 15–49 years.[5] But with better living standards and improved health services, female mortality has declined over the years. The decline is largely contributed by the drop in maternal mortality.

Figure 4.1
Expectation Of Life At Birth By Ethnic Group For Males In Peninsular Malaysia, 1957–1987

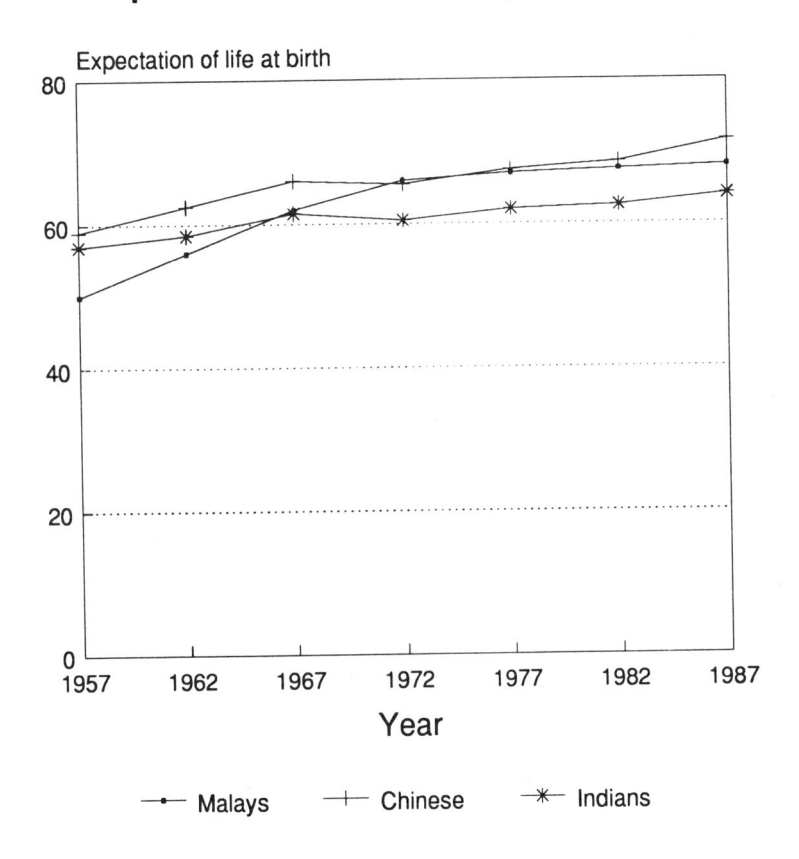

●— Malays   +— Chinese   *— Indians

Source: Abridged Life Tables—Vital Statistics, various years. Tan Poo Chang, et. al., (1989), Figure 2a.

Figure 4.2
Expectation Of Life At Birth By Ethnic Group For Females In Peninsular Malaysia, 1957–1987

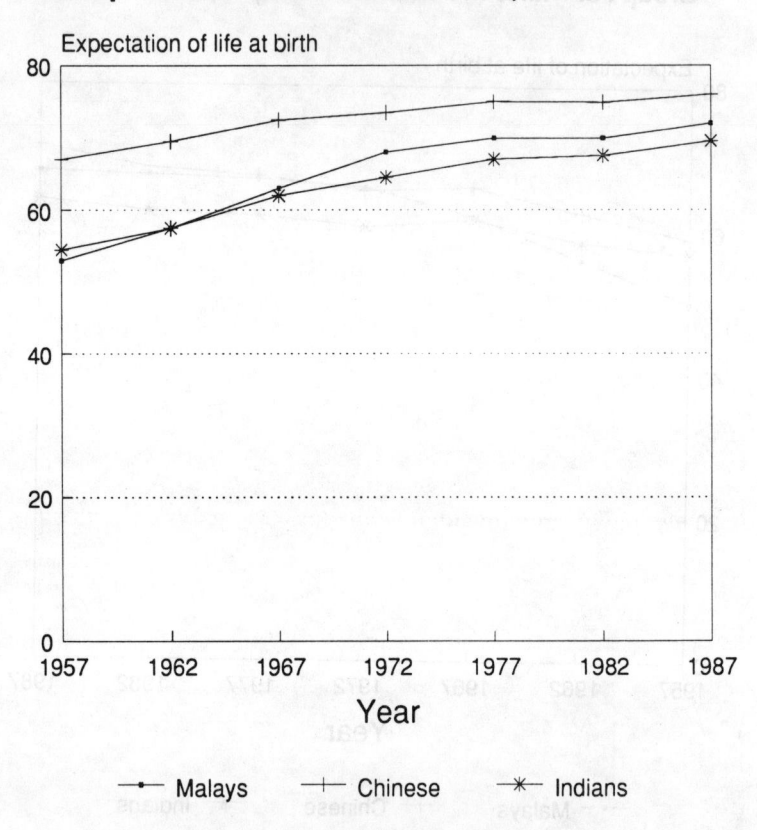

Source: Abridged Life Tables—Vital Statistics, various years. Tan Poo Chang, et. al., (1989), Figure 1b.

Figure 4.3
Age-Specific Death Rate By Ethnic Group For Males In Peninsular Malaysia, 1984–1986

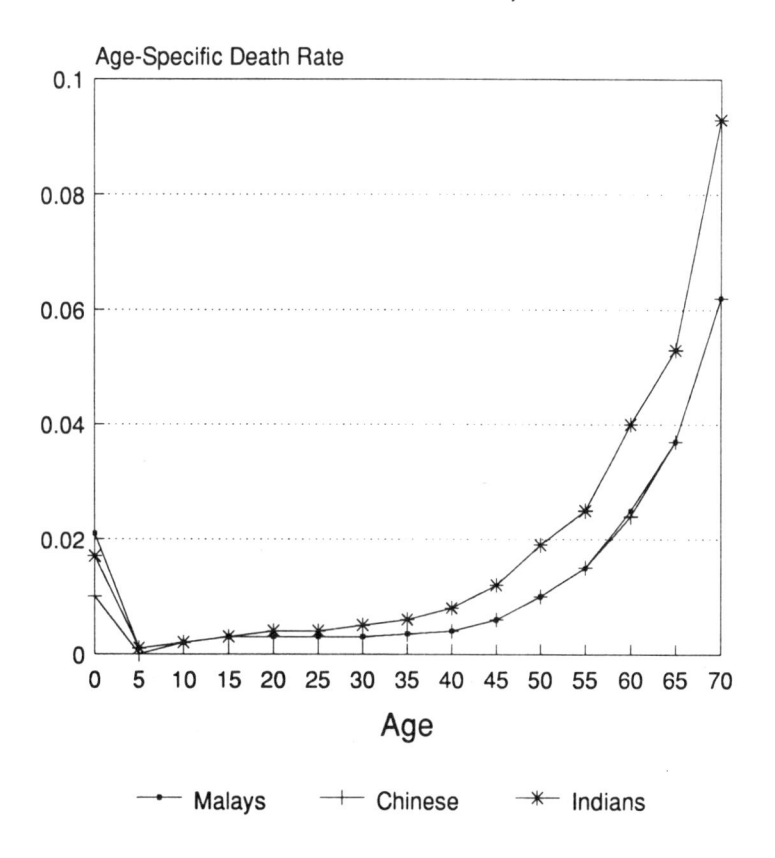

Source: Abridged Life Tables, 1987: 31–35. Tan Poo Chang, et. al., Figure 3a.

Figure 4.4
Age-Specific Death Rate By Ethnic Group For Females In Peninsular Malaysia, 1984–1986

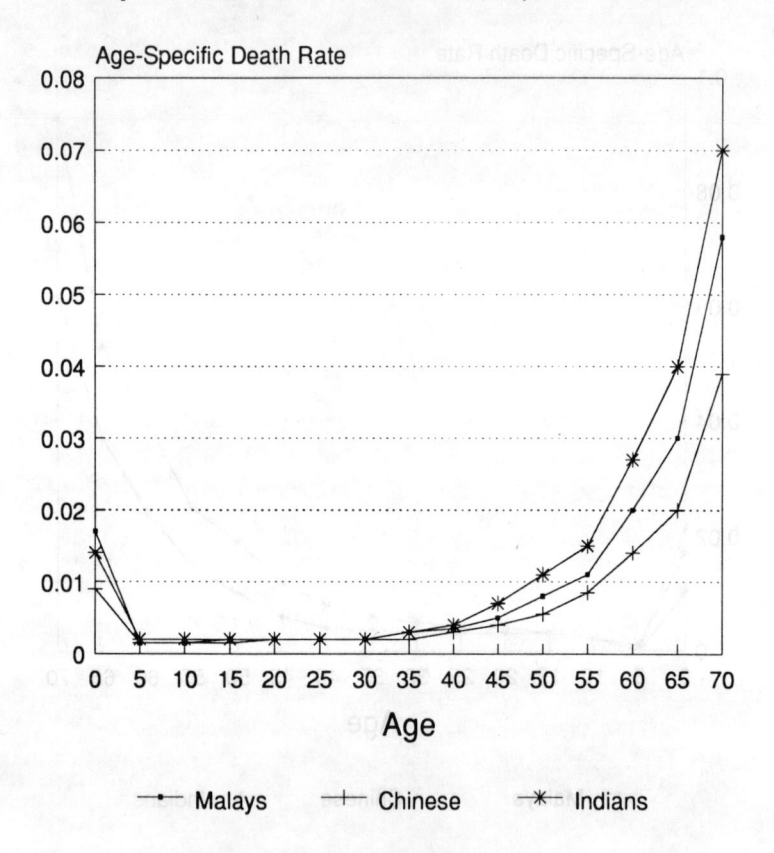

Source: Abridged Life Tables, 1987: 31–35. Tan Poo Chang, et. al., (1989), Figure 3b.

Maternal Mortality

Maternal mortality is defined as the number of mothers who died as a result of complications during pregnancy and delivery.[6] It accounts for the largest proportion of deaths among women of reproductive age in most developing countries, including Malaysia. Table 4.1 shows that maternal mortality had declined sharply for all ethnic groups between 1966 and 1986. Compared to the Chinese, the Malay and Indian mothers had rates of more than two and one per thousand respectively in 1970.[7] In 1986, the Chinese mothers were still in a better position with a relatively low mortality rate. The data here indicate the need to work towards improving the living standards and health facilities of the Indian and Malay women.

Table 4.1
**Maternal Mortality Rate by Ethnic Group,
Peninsular Malaysia, 1966–1986**

Year	Malays	Chinese	Indians	Total
1966	n.a.	n.a	n.a.	1.79
1970	2.15	0.46	1.16	1.48
1975	1.21	0.19	0.63	0.83
1980	0.89	0.13	0.43	0.63
1983	0.53	0.13	0.17	0.40
1986	0.37	0.08	0.25	0.30

Note: n.a. = not available. Total includes other ethnic groups.
Source: Vital Statistics, various years. Department of Statistics, Malaysia.

Infant Mortality

Maternal health and the health and survival of children are interrelated. Nearly one-fifth of all infant deaths usually occur in the first month of life and this can be traced to problems such as maternal health, nutritional status, care during pregnancy and delivery, number of children and spacing between children.

Infant mortality can be categorized into two groups—the neonatal and the post-neonatal. Neonatal deaths are those that occur within 28 days of birth while post-neonatal deaths include those that occur within the period after four weeks of birth to before one year after birth.[8]

Table 4.2
Selected Reproductive And Socio-Economic Indicators By Ethnic Group

Ethnic Group	Perinatal Mortality Rate	% Low Birth Rate	%* With Known Birth Weight	% Urban	%+ With No Education	%+ With Primary School Education
	1986	1986	1986	1980	1980	1980
Malays	19.4	8.8	39.9	14.0	21.3	39.9
Chinese	11.2	6.3	56.9	18.7	18.0	41.8
Indians	21.9	15.2	55.7	4.1	22.0	40.9

* Live birth only
+ Women of age 15–49 years

Source: 1986 Vital Statistics and 1980 Population and Housing Census. Taken from Tan Poo Chang, 1989.

The three ethnic groups in Peninsular Malaysia recorded a decline in both the neonatal and post-neonatal mortality rates for the period 1957–1987. The Malays showed the largest decline in neonatal rates, while decline in the post-neonatal rates for the Malays and Chinese were similar and larger than that of the Indians. Generally, the post-neonatal mortality levels fell faster than the neonatal mortality levels for all three ethnic groups.

Deaths are more apparent in the early neonatal period than the late neonatal period. Therefore the perinatal mortality rate is often used to measure neonatal mortality.[9] Perinatal mortality rate combines still births or deaths after 28 weeks of gestation and deaths during the first week.

Perinatal mortality rates declined over the period of 20 years, from 1966–1986. The male rates were higher than the female rates and the Chinese again were in a better position than the Indians and Malays, with a much lower perinatal mortality rate.

Available data also indicate that the perinatal mortality rates are highest in groups with low socio-economic status. This is not surprising as such groups lack access to health services and facilities. High perinatal mortality rates are closely linked to low birth weights of babies among these people. To bring about a reduction in perinatal mortality rates would require efforts towards improving standards of living and greater utilization of health facilities.

It is important that women, especially mothers-to-be, obtain knowledge on childcare, and instill in themselves nutritional and health values. This can be achieved through proper education. However, in 1980, 40% of women aged between 15 to 49 years had only primary education while 21% were without education.[10] These data also indicate that a large proportion of married women have low education as they usually drop out after completing their primary education. The poor educational level of the mothers is responsible for their ignorance in health issues such as how to seek medical help and treatment.

Low birth weight is one of the major contributors to infant mortality. Multiple factors in the mother, such as age, parity, height, socio-economic status, past obstetric history and smoking habits are likely to be interdependent in their influence on pregnancy outcome and birth weight. Amongst these factors, women over 35 years of age, who have had four or more children, who are less educated and with poor health and nutritional status are more likely to have low birth weight babies.

Figure 4.5
Infant Mortality Rate By Ethnic Group For Peninsular Malaysia, 1957–1987

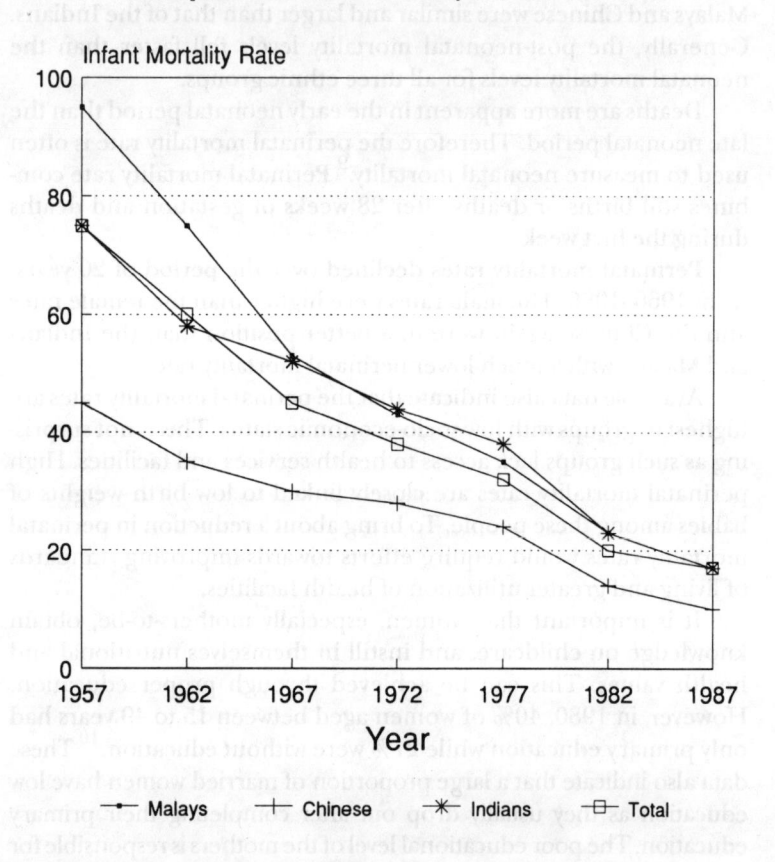

Source: Vital Statistics, various years. Tan Poo Chang, et. al., (1989), Figure 4.

Figure 4.6
Perinatal Mortality Rate And Its Components For Peninsular Malaysia, 1966–1986

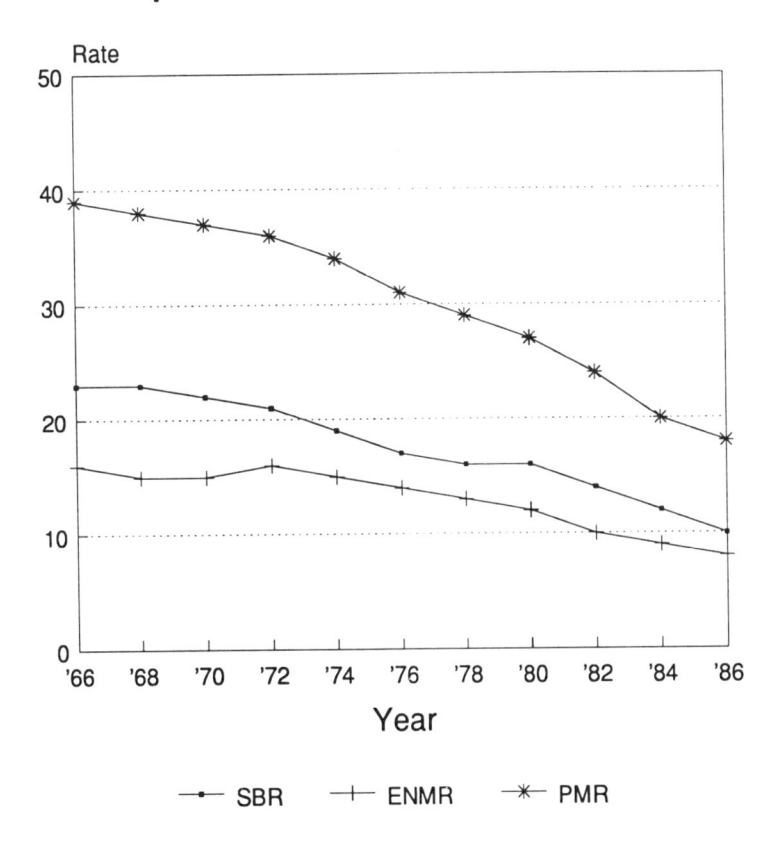

SBR—Stillbirth Rate
ENMR—Early Neonatal Mortality Rate
PMR—Perinatal Mortality Rate

Source: Vital Statistics, various years. Tan Poo Chang, et. al., (1989), Figure 6.

Table 4.3
Expectation Of Life At Birth For Males And Females Among Selected Countries In Asia, 1986

Country	Male	Female
Asean Countries		
Singapore	70	75
Malaysia	67	71
Philippines	62	65
Thailand	62	66
Indonesia	55	58
Other Developing Countries In Asia		
Sri Lanka	68	72
People's Republic of China	68	70
India	57	56
Pakistan	52	51
Bangladesh	51	50
Nepal	48	47
Developed Countries In Asia		
Japan	75	81
Hong Kong	73	79
Republic of Korea	66	73
Countries In Oceania		
Australia	75	80
New Zealand	71	77

Source: World Development Report, 1988: 286–287. Tan Poo Chang, 1989.

Table 4.4
Mortality Indicators By Selected Countries

Country	Maternal Mortality Per 100,000 Live Births 1980	Infant Mortality Per 1,000 Live Births 1965	Infant Mortality Per 1,000 Live Births 1986
Asean Countries			
Singapore	11	26	9
Malaysia	59	55	27
Philippines	80	72	46
Thailand	270	88	41
Indonesia	800	136	87
Other Developing Countries In Asia			
Sri Lanka	90	63	29
China	44	90	34
India	500	151	86
Pakistan	600	149	111
Bangladesh	600	153	121
Nepal	850	184	130
Developed Countries In Asia			
Japan	15	18	6
Hong Kong	6	28	8
Republic of Korea	34	63	25
Countries In Oceania			
Australia	11	19	10
New Zealand	14	20	11

Source: *World Development Report 1988: 286–287.* Tan Poo Chang, 1989.

Higher infant mortality rate is also due to short pregnancy intervals. Available statistics show that this trend prevails among Indian mothers. Short intervals cause gestational prematurity which is related to lower birth-weight, nutritional deficiency of the mother or competition of a previous young and surviving infant for the mother's attention.[11]

Compared to neighbouring countries as well as other developing and developed nations, Malaysia has achieved a relatively high expectation of life at birth for males and females. (See Table 4.3). Malaysia is placed second after Singapore as having one of the lowest maternal and infant mortality rates. (See Table 4.4). In fact Malaysia is in a much better position than many other developing countries in Asia such as Sri Lanka, India, China and Pakistan, and is not very far behind the developed countries in its record of low mortality rates.

Nevertheless, the country still needs to look into the disparity in mortality rates between ethnic groups. Factors such as the differences in economic status and socio-cultural practices that contribute towards the disparity should be studied. There is still room for improvement in the case of the Malay and Indian mothers. The other area of concern is the high death risk among very young children. Related to this is the low educational levels of the mothers. Therefore, there is a need to work towards educating mothers to ensure that they are capable of providing adequate health care to their young for their survival.

Fertility Trends

Fertility changes are closely related to marriage patterns, contraceptive use and the socio-economic status of women in terms of education and work participation.

Malaysia is said to be experiencing a population growth rate of 2% in the late 1980s. The growth can be attributed to natural increase of births minus deaths.[12] The trend of high births and low deaths in the 1950s and early 1960s later changed to that characterized by a gradual decline in both birth and death rates in the late 1960s and early 1970s. This section of the chapter will probe into the fertility changes in relation to marriage patterns, contraceptive use and women's status in Malaysia.

Changes in the fertility and mortality rates from high to low can be attributed to economic and social development. According to

Coale and Hoover (1959) "... as the economy changes from an agrarian to a more independent and specialized market economy, death rates decline and will continue to do so when there is better organization and improved medical care."[13] Although in most countries decline in birth rates is much slower than death rates, the general pattern is towards that of small families.

The incidence of high fertility rates is still very much a problem in many developing countries. However, countries like Malaysia and Singapore are exceptional cases. Based on a study conducted by Bernard and Berelson (1978) and Cho and Palmer (1967), fertility decline in West Malaysia in the 1960s was mainly attributed to change in factors such as age-structure, marriage patterns and marital fertility. Of the three factors, the rising age at marriage has the greatest impact on fertility decline in West Malaysia.[14] Improvement in women's socio-economic status is the main reason for the rise in age at marriage.

Marriage Patterns And Fertility Trends

Marriage and fertility are interrelated in Malaysia as strict social and cultural norms do not permit births outside marriage although illegitimate births do occur.[15] Marriage is thus a vital factor in fertility as it leads to sexual unions and exposure to conception. Marriage can affect fertility through age of entry into sexual unions, permanent celibacy, periods of divorce or separation and widowhood.[16]

According to Malaysian civil law, the minimum age requirement for marriage is 16 years for women and 18 years for men. The mean age at first marriage has increased for both men and women. The mean age at first marriage for men was 23.8 years in 1957 and this rose to 25.8 years in 1980. For women, the mean age at first marriage was 19.4 years in 1957 and it has increased to 22.8 years in 1980. (See Table 4.5). This trend is notably present among the Chinese compared to the Indians and Malays. (See Table 4.6).

By referring once again to the socio-economic status of women it is apparent that education is positively linked to the mean age at first marriage. Data in Table 4.7 show that women with no education married at age 16.7 years whilst those with more than twelve years of education married at 22.4 years. A similar trend is seen in the relationship between the working status and the age at first marriage. Working women marry at a much later age compared to those who do not work. (See Table 4.8).

Table 4.5
Mean Age At First Marriage Of Women 10 Years And Over For The Years 1957, 1970 And 1980 For Peninsular Malaysia

	Year		
Sex	1957	1970	1980
Male	23.8	25.8	26.9
Female	19.4	22.3	23.8

Source: Calculated from Population Census, 1957, 1970 and 1980. Masitah Mohd. Yatim, "Development Process and Malaysian Female Fertility: A Macro Level Analysis of Trends and Patterns", 1957–1987. [Colloquium on Women and Development in Malaysia].

Table 4.6
Mean Age At First Marriage By Ethnic Groups For All Ever Married Women Aged 25 Years And Above Who Were Married Before Age 25.

Ethnic Group	All Women	Current Age 25–29	Current Age 45 and over
Malays	16.6	17.7	15.7
Chinese	19.6	20.7	18.4
Indians	17.1	17.9	17.1
Others	19.6**	*	*

* Less than 20 cases
** Less than 50 cases

Source: MFFS 1974. Masitah Mohd. Yatim, " Development Process and Malaysian Female Fertility: A Macro Level Analysis of Trends and Patterns, 1957–1987. [Colloquium on Women and Development in Malaysia].

Table 4.7
Mean Age At First Marriage By Educational Level
For Ever-Married Women Aged 25 Years And Above Who
Were Married Before Age 25

Educational Level	All Ages	25–29	Mean Age At First Marriage 45 And Over
No Education	16.7	17.5	16.2
Formal Education			
Less than 7 years	17.9	18.4	17.3
7 to 12 years	20.8	21.3	18.7
More than 12 years	22.4**	22.5**	*

* Less than 20 cases
** Less than 50 cases

Table 4.8
Mean Age At First Marriage By Work Status
And Selected Occupation For All Ever-Married Women
Who Were Married Before The Age Of 25

Work Status Before First Marriage	All Women	Current Age 25–29	Current Age 45 and Over
Not working	17.0	18.0	16.5
Unpaid family worker	16.8	18.1	16.3
Own-account worker	18.0	18.8	17.1
Employee	19.2	19.9	17.9
Total	**17.6**	**18.8**	**16.7**

Source: Malaysian Family and Fertility Survey, 1974. Masitah Mohd. Yatim, 1989.

Early marriage allows longer exposure to pregnancy. However, the number of children a woman can have depends on the number of fertile years she has for childbearing. Although delayed marriage results in the delay of births, but not necessarily the number of children ever born.[17] It is also the time spent in a married state that determines the risk of exposure to conception.[18] Therefore, fertility is affected by divorce, separation and widowhood. Among the different ethnic groups in Malaysia, the Malays have the highest record of the number of divorces (Malaysian Population and Family Survey, 1984), yet fertility rate is highest among them. This could be due to low contraceptive use within this group.

Contraceptive Use And Fertility Trends

The use of contraceptives as part of the family planning method has been one of the most important factor in determining the size of the family. Family planning activities in Malaysia became more intense and organized with the establishment of the Family Planning Board in 1967.[19] In 1984, the Board took a new name and is now known as the Population and Family Development Board. Nevertheless, family planning remains as one of its main activities.

Table 4.9
Percentage Of Currently Married Women Using Various Contraceptive Methods In 196/67, 1970 And 1974

Contraceptive Method Used	1974	1970	1966/67
Proportion of currently married women using contraceptives	35.5	16.1	8.8
Total	100.0	100.0	100.0
	(1,797)	(2,744)	(476)
Pill	50.7	75.3	46.4
IUD	2.2	*	2.3
Condom	9.1	*	9.0
Other female methods	0.4	*	1.9
Sterilization	10.6	*	*
Rhythm	10.8	24.7	*
Withdrawal	5.7	*	40.4
Abstinence	4.3	*	*
Other folk methods	6.2	*	*

Figures in parentheses ( ) indicate the number of respondents.
* Data on the detailed breakdown of some of the methods used were not available in 1966/67 and 1970 Surveys. Note that, for comparative purposes, the data are confined to currently married women of 15 to 44 years of age.

Source: Malaysian Fertility and Family Survey, 1974. Masitah Mohd. Yatim, 1989.

Table 4.9(a)
Percent Distribution Of Currently Married Women By Currently Using Contraceptives By Ethnic Groups, 1984

Ethnic Group	Currently Using	Not Using	Total
Malays	864	602	1,466
	(58.9)	(41.1)	(100)
Chinese	856	314	1,170
	(73.2)	(26.8)	(100)
Indians	259	62	321
	(80.7)	(19.3)	(100)
Others	19	11	30
	(63.3)	(36.7)	(100)
Total	1,998	989	2,987
	(66.9)	(33.1)	(100)

Figures in parentheses ( ) denote percentages.

Source: Malaysian Population and Family Survey, 1984.

WOMEN IN MEDICINE 95

Table 4.9(b)
Percentage Of Currently Married Non-Pregnant Women Currently Using Contraceptive Methods By Seleceted Background Variables And Number Of Living Children, 1974

Characteristics	Total	Number Of Living Children				
		0	1	2	3	4 or More
Educational Level						
All women	38.0	8.6	34.1	40.4	42.5	40.4
No education	24.8	2.6	10.5	12.2	24.2	24.7
Less than 7 years	42.2	4.4	34.0	41.0	45.7	48.6
7 to 12 years	55.9	21.0	47.3	64.4	67.0	68.1
More than 12 years	73.2	*	*	*	*	*
Standardized for education	38.0	6.2	27.9	34.4	41.7	44.0
Ethnic Group						
Malays	26.1	3.5	24.0	26.8	30.1	28.4
Chinese	55.1	21.3	48.5	60.5	58.9	56.7
Indians	48.9	8.7**	42.5**	47.1	47.3	54.4

* Less than 20 cases
** Less than 50 cases

Source: Malaysian Fertility and Family Survey, 1974. Masitah Mohd. Yatim, 1989.

According to the Population and Family Survey of 1984, 66.9% of married women were using contraceptives. There is a definite increase in the percentage of currently married women using various contraceptive methods, as shown in Table 4.9. The Malays registered the lowest percentage practising family planning. [See Table 4.9(a)]. Education too seems to have an influence in the use of contraceptives. Data from Table 4.9(b) show that only 24.8% of currently married women with no education use contraceptives compared to 73.2% of those with more than twelve years of education. From available data on the age-specific fertility rates, it is apparent that there is a positive relationship between change in attitude towards family size and contraceptive use. All three ethnic groups display a trend towards smaller families, with the Chinese having a higher decline rate than Malays and Indians. This in turn suggests that the Chinese are also the highest contraceptive users.

Fertility Trends And The Status Of Women

With rapid socio-economic development since its independence in 1957, women in Malaysia too have experienced changes in their status. They now have access to almost all the social, political and economic activities of the country. Higher education and increasing employment opportunities have provided them with an alternative to their traditional role of wife, mother and unpaid worker.

Women's progress in areas such as education, labour force, politics and health have contributed towards their longer life expectancy at birth (that is, 72 years) and also the decline in infant and maternal mortality. Similarly, their improved status in society is closely linked to the decline in their fertility. It is found that better educated women and those with careers have lower fertility than the less educated and non-working women. Findings of the Malaysian Population and Family Survey (1985) have proven this to be true.

The Chinese women who generally are relatively of a higher socio-economic status are influenced by both education and work opportunities in their family planning practices. The desired number of children decreases with higher levels of education and also better work opportunities.[20] With education, priority is given to improving the standard of living and quality of life for both children and the family at large.

WOMEN'S ACCESS TO HEALTH FACILITIES AND MATERNAL CARE SERVICES

Development Of The Health Care System

The health care system in Malaysia consists of two major sectors—the Government and the private sector. The distribution of Government health and medical services was inequitable under the colonial rule.[21] Health facilities were primarily located in urban areas and the development of medical services for the rural inhabitants were neglected. However, in 1954, a rural health service programme was initiated to upgrade the health services in the rural areas. Maternity care was one of the four major services provided through this programme. After Independence, more emphasis was given to develop the maternal and child health services in rural areas. In the 1960s, rural health service infrastructure was provided with a comprehensive range of services and an emphasis on maternal and child health services. From the 1960s onwards, Rural Health Services was formulated with the First Malaya Plan and it was further developed with the subsequent development plans. In the mid-1970s, the provision of maternal health care facilities and services was expanded to more backward areas and disadvantaged groups. At the same time, attempts were made to improve existing health services in those areas. Among some of the improvements made were the upgrading of personnel and the provision of full-time doctors in health centres.

The Primary Health Care Survey (1980) discovered that only 7% of the rural population in Peninsular Malaysia did not have access to health facilities within a radius of five kilometers. Through the expansion of the rural health services, a wider scope of sevices was made available to a larger proportion of the population. The progress made in providing health and medical facilities is shown in Table 4.10.

Provision Of Maternal Health Care

The maternal health care services consist of activities such as antenatal care, domiciliary delivery, postnatal care and family planning. They are aimed at promoting and maintaining the health of the mother and her family. The Ministry of Health is the main provider of maternal health care in Malaysia. Various sectors, such as the Rural Health Services (health centres and mobile services),

Government general and district hospitals and polyclinics, private and estate hospitals, maternity homes; the Population and Family Development Board; local authorities in Kuala Lumpur, Penang, Ipoh and Malacca; and other sectors such as the University Hospital, Orang Asli Department, Police, Army, etc., form part of the network of the Malaysian medical and health infrastructure.[22]

Table 4.10
**Progress In Development Of
Physical Health Facilities, Peninsular Malaysia**

	1976	1987
General Hospitals	12	12
District Hospitals	46	52
Main Health centres	39	149
Health Sub centres	122	236
Maternal and Child Health Centres	–	56
Midwives Clinics	643	829
Klinik Desas	–	800
Number of maternity beds in Government Hospitals	2,292 (1973)	–

Source: Dr. Raj Karim, "Impact of Government Medical and Health Facilities on the Status of Maternal Health in Malaysia. [Colloquium on Women and Development in Malaysia] 1989.

Maternal health services are made available in both urban and rural areas. Rural inhabitants have access to health centres, village and midwife clinics. For the more remote inhabitants, maternal health care and basic health services are provided by mobile health teams by road, river or air. In urban areas, maternal health care is obtainable in district and general hospitals, private hospitals and maternity homes.[23]

It would not be sufficient to merely improve the health and medical infrastructure. Maternal health care with its wide range of activities involves various groups of trained personnel such as doctors, medical assistants, nursing personnel that include matrons, sisters, public health nurses, staff nurses, assistant nurses, midwives, village nurses and family planning workers.[24]

Doctors from both the government and private sectors are the main leading providers of maternal health care in urban areas. On the other hand, nurses and midwives play a vital role in the health care system of rural areas. The Ministry of Health is not only taking steps towards increasing the number of nurses in health centres, but also in upgrading the quality of personnel by providing proper training.

Traditional birth attendants or village midwives are an important group in the provision of maternal health care in Malaysia. They provide for the socio-cultural and religious needs of the woman and her family. Presently (1989), there are 1,767 registered and 2,447 unregistered traditional birth attendants in the country.[25]

Impact Of Maternal Health Care On Mortality Rates

Maternal health care is vital for the survival and health of infants and mothers. Progress made in providing extensive maternal health care and health facilities has contributed to the overall decline in mortality rates. In 1987, more than 90% of women in the country as well as those in the rural areas received some form of antenatal care. The frequency of visits made to pregnant women in rural areas has also increased over the last ten years. As a result, the percentage of safe deliveries increased to 88.4% with a total of 429,847 live births.[26]

Improved medical and health infrastructure led to a change of place of delivery with an increasing preference for institutions, especially among the urban and semi-urban population. Some of the reasons for the shift were the lack of space at home,[27] no home help and fear of arising complications at home (Study conducted by the Ministry of Health on the Preference of Place of Delivery among Pregnant Women in Selangor and Kuala Lumpur, 1985). With this change of place of delivery, the high risk of maternal deaths arising from serious complications during delivery could be minimized.

Maternal mortality is also due to women whose deliveries are attended to by untrained personnel or traditional midwives. Studies conducted in Kedah and Pulau Pinang revealed that the rural Malay community still prefers traditional methods of delivery by traditional midwives. To reduce deaths among the community, the Government has made efforts to register the traditional midwives and also provide training to upgrade their skills and knowledge.

Among the main causes of maternal mortality are post-partum haemorrhage, infection and associated medical complications.[28] Problems such as lack of awareness among women on the importance of regular antenatal care, preference for home deliveries by traditional midwives, refusal of hospital admission, poor hygienic practices in the home, being pregnant too often and at close intervals are some of the causes of maternal mortality.[29] Since 1986, the Ministry of Health has launched a national effort to tackle these problems. Efforts include improving health facilities in the district hospitals, upgrading skills of health workers, motivating high-risk women to deliver in hospitals and introducing family planning methods.

It can be said that as a result of the availability and accessibility of medical and health facilities, mortality rates have declined. An indicator of the improvement in the status of maternal health is that life expectancy of women exceeded life expectancy of men in 1986. The infant mortality rate, which is a rough indicator of the general health status of a country, has also declined from 102 per 1,000 live births in 1947 to 16.9 per 1,000 in 1985.[30]

PARTICIPATION OF WOMEN IN MEDICINE

There are two ways in which women encounter the medical system: as workers in that system and as consumers of the care and services it delivers. In this section of the chapter we will analyse women's participation as workers in the health care system. Gender stereotyping deems women as suitable for the caring and nurturing professions. Apart from the education sector, health is perhaps the only other sector which has an overwhelming female participation.

Thirty years ago, there were only 55 local women doctors who were registered with the Malaysian Medical Council. More than 85% of the doctors then were men. It was only in the mid-1960s that women's participation in the medical field showed some improvement. With increasing education opportunities for women, more and more women enrolled in medical schools. By 1988, 24.8% of the total 6,274 medical practitioners were women.[31] The majority of women doctors are now practising in urban areas.

Related to this is the dominance of women doctors in Government service. Forty-nine per cent of doctors in the Government service comprise women. On the contrary, only 26.6% are male doctors.

A 10-year follow-up study conducted in Universiti Kebangsaan Malaysia (See Sharifah, 1989, p. 25) reveals that women medical students possess relatively excellent academic achievements. However, there are still very few women specialists. Only 15.9% of those classified as specialists by the Medical Council were women. In descending order of popularity they were found mostly in the Public Health, Pathology, Paediatrics, Internal Medicine, Obstetrics and Gynaecology, Microbiology, Radiology, Ophthalmology, Anaesthesiology, Psychiatry and Surgery.[32] This trend shows that women are less inclined or motivated, compared to men, in acquiring additional qualifications.

Women are very well represented in the allied health professions such as nursing, midwifery, physiotherapy, occupational therapy and radiography. They are the ancillary workers in the health care system. Stereotyped opinions of females being passive, non-objective and prey to emotional and hormonal disturbances, discriminate against and prevent women from holding jobs with any real authority within the health care system. For example, 99% of the nurses in Malaysia are women. Furthermore, women doctors are found in their highest numbers either in the specialities with a more nurturing, caring type of orientation, or else involved with children. For instance, women's involvement in surgical-based specialities is still insignificant. In addition, few women hold top decision-making posts in the medical-service system.

As in other specialized medical fields, women's participation in obstetrics and gynaecology[33] is low. Although obstetricians and gynaecologists are considered as experts on the subject of women's reproductive functions and related illnesses there are very few women qualified in this field. However, at this stage, it is impossible to make a conclusive remark on this issue as data on women's participation in this field are rather scarce.

Historically, women were the recognized healers and bearers of society's medical knowledge. In Europe, knowledgeable women, often labelled as "witches", also acted as abortionists, nurses, midwives, pharmacists and councillors. The advent of medical schools and the expansion of scientific medicine paved the way for the displacement of the witches and midwives by the male obstetricians.

Whereas within the Malaysian society, the traditional midwives in the Malay health system are fortunately, still practising their skills, especially in rural areas. The introduction of the Supplementary Register for the purpose of registering traditional midwives with the Government health care system has helped to facilitate their training and supervision. Their presence is vital for the maternal care of women in rural areas where it is impossible to provide modern health facilities to every resident.

CONCLUSION

The health care system cannot be separated from the general political, cultural and economic systems in which we live. It cannot also be isolated from the roles we are playing and the status we have in the society. Viewed within this context, enlightened Government health care systems must ensure that women's interests should be safeguarded. This is necessary especially in countries which are traditionally patriarchal male-dominated societies.

It is undeniable that when compared to several other developing countries, Malaysia has a good health care system and has made impressive progress in mortality and fertility reduction. Increasing education and occupation opportunities for women have helped to improve their attitude and awareness on maternal and child health care and efficient family planning. Nevertheless, there is still much to be done. Existing social class and ethnic disparity in mortality and fertility rates calls for greater efforts to look into strategies that will rectify the unequal situation. Special consideration should be given to socio-cultural factors affecting health care practices among the ethnic groups. This is essential as the disparity can be attributed to the differentials in economic status of the different groups.

Another aspect that needs looking into is the availability and accessibility of health facilities and maternal care services. There is no doubt that improved modern health facilities in both the government and private sectors have contributed towards the drop in mortality and fertility levels. Expansion of these facilities and services in rural areas has reduced the imbalanced distribution between the rural and urban areas that have been prevailing since colonial times. For future advancement in health and maternal care, more women need to be educated and made much more aware of basic health care and nutrition.

With regard to women's participation in medicine, there has been a notable increase of women doctors since the mid-1960s. This trend can be attributed to the improved education opportunities for women in Malaysia which have lead to the increasing enrolment of female students in medical schools. However, women doctors are still lagging in their career advancement as compared to their male counterparts. Relatively very few women have acquired specialist status. It is also the men doctors who still dominate the positions of authority and decision-making in the medical service system.

As emphasized at the beginning of this chapter, it is particularly the childbearing role and nurturing ability of women that make it very necessary for them to have contact with the medical service. Clearly, if women have to play a more effective role in the nation's development, more attention must be given to women's health status and their effective participation in medicine as well as a greater say in health policy-making decisions.

NOTES

[1] Tan Poo Chang, *et al.*, "Sex Differentials and Mortality Trends in the Process of Development in Malaysia," *Women and Development in Malaysia—Implications for Planning and Population Dynamics*, p. 5.
[2] Tan, *et al.*, p. 5
[3] Tan, *et al.*, p. 5
[4] Tan, *et al.*, p. 6
[5] Tan, *et al.*, p. 9
[6] Tan, *et al.*, p. 13
[7] Tan, *et al.*, p. 13
[8] Tan, *et al.*, p. 13
[9] Tan, *et al.*, p. 17
[10] Tan, *et al.*, p. 19
[11] Tan, *et al.*, p. 23
[12] Masitah Mohd. Yatim, "Development Process of Malaysian Female Fertility: A Macro-Level Analysis of Trends and Patterns, 1957–1987", *Women and Development in Malaysia—Implications for Planning and Population Dynamics*, p. 1
[13] Masitah, p. 2
[14] Masitah, p. 5.
[15] Masitah, p. 5.

[16] Masitah, p. 5.
[17] Masitah, p. 10.
[18] Masitah, p. 10.
[19] Masitah, p. 13.
[20] Masitah, p. 21.
[21] Sharifah Hapsah Shahabudin, "Women in the Medical and Health Professions", *Women and Development in Malaysia— Implications for Planning and Population Dynamics*, p. 6.
[22] Raj Karim, Dr., "Impact of Government Medical and Health Facilities on the Status of Maternal Health in Malaysia", *Women and Development in Malaysia—Implications for Planning and Population Dynamics*, p. 5.
[23] Raj, p. 6.
[24] Raj, p. 7.
[25] Raj, p. 7.
[26] Raj, p. 13.
[27] Raj, p. 14.
[28] Raj, p. 16.
[29] Raj, p. 16.
[30] Sharifah, Dr., p. 3.
[31] Sharifah, Dr., p. 1.
[32] Sharifah, Dr., p. 24.
[33] According to *The Collins Paperback English Dictionary*, Obstetrics is the branch of medicine concerned with childbirth and the treatment of women before and after childbirth while Gynaecology is the branch of medicine concerned with the diseases of women.

BIBLIOGRAPHY

Chee, Heng Leng, *The Development of Health Care Systems in Malaysia: Achievements and Shortfalls*, December 1988, Department of Statistics, Malaysia (various years), Vital Statistics.

Malaysian Medical Association, *The Future of the Health Services in Malaysia*, 1980.

Malaysian Population and Family Survey, 1984, *National Population and Family Development Board Malaysia*.

Masitah Mohd. Yatim, "Development Process and Malaysian Female Fertility—A Macro Level Analysis of Trends and Patterns, 1957–1987". Paper presented at the Population Studies Colloquium on *Women and Development in Malaysia—Implications for Planning and Population Dynamics,* January 1989.

Nik Safiah Karim, Dr., "Wanita Malaysia Sebelum dan Sesudah Dekad Wanita". Unpublished paper presented at the seminar on *The Period of Women's Achievement and Challenges,* Kuala Lumpur, August 1985.

Noor Laily binti Abu Bakar, Datin, *et al.,* "The Changing Ethnic Pattern of Mortality in Malaysia, 1957-1979", *National Family Planning Board Research Paper,* No. 6, February 1983.

Raj Karim, Dr., "Impact of Government Medical and Health Facilities on the Status of Maternal Health in Malaysia". Paper presented at the Population Studies Colloquium on *Women and Development in Malaysia—Implications for Planning and Population Dynamics,* University of Malaya, January 1989.

Sharifah Hapsah Shahabudin, Dr., "Women in the Medical and Health Professions". Paper presented at the Population Studies Colloquium on *Women and Development in Malaysia—Implications for Planning and Population Dynamics,* January 1989.

Tan, Poo Chang, *et al.,* "Sex Differentials and Mortality Trends in the Process of Development in Malaysia". Paper presented at the Population Studies Colloquium on *Women and Development in Malaysia—Implications for Planning and Population Dynamics,* January 1989.

Tan, P.C., *et al.,* "Socio-economic Development and Mortality Patterns and Trends in Malaysia", *Asia Pacific Population Journal,* Vol. 2, No. 1: 3-20, 1980.

5
Women In Organized Movements And Government Service

Historically, the public arena of politics and government of Malaysia has always been dominated by men. In this chapter, we will be tracing the growth of women's organized movement in Malaysia and their participation in government and its administration. Part One looks at the trend and orientation of women's organized movement, Part Two provides some details on women politics and Part Three deals with women's participation in the government service.

PART I:
THE TREND AND ORIENTATION OF WOMEN'S ORGANIZED MOVEMENTS

The beginnings of women's mass movement in Malaysia germinated after the Second World War as an off-shoot of the anti-colonial, nationalist movement. Two prominent groups were the Angkatan Wanita Sedar (AWAS) formed in 1946 and the Kaum Ibu, organized in 1949. As mentioned in Chapter One, AWAS was led by the left wing members of the Malay Nationalist Party. Among its main objectives, it aimed to make Malay women more conscious of their political rights. Its leaders include Shamsiah Fakeh, Sakinah Junid and Zainab Baginda. AWAS succeeded in gaining the support from women of the peasantry as well as the Malay rural gentry. However, its growing strength was suppressed by the colonial administration and consequently it was banned. Internal discord amongst its members led to its final disintegration. The other group was the Kaum Ibu, which as described in Chapter One, started off as a women's voluntary association, essentially as a mother's club and played a supportive role to the men in the Malay nationalist movement. It therefore did not focus on women's political issues and strived to reinforced Malay women's nurturing role as good mothers and homemakers. However, eventually, with encouragement from the men leaders, who foresaw the strategic advantage of involving women's mass participation, Kaum Ibu changed its name to Wanita Umno, hence becoming a full-fledged women's political organization. Indeed, by the change in its name, it has broadened its objectives as well as its scope such as to include non-married women members. However, it must be noted that it was accorded a status which was equal to the male Youth's wing of UMNO but secondary to the men's wing. This *status quo* remains unchanged to the present day.

Both AWAS and Kaum Ibu impressed the British colonial Administration that they were a political force to be reckoned with through their active supportive role in rallying mass support during the nationalist movement and subsequently in the struggle for Independence. They were also active campaigners and reliable voters in the first national elections.

During this time, the women from the other ethnic groups were not active in political parties, other than those who participated in the anti-Japanese underground movement and pro-communist insurgencies. It was only recently, in the 1970s, that Chinese and Indian women formed the women's wing of MCA and MIC respectively. Women's organizations of the other political parties like WANITA GERAKAN, WANITA DAP, and the women's section of PAS also came into existence during this period.

Generally, the women's voluntary associations of that post-World War Two era, were comprised mainly of elite women's group and expatriate wives. They focused on women's roles in the home and in social welfare. Some examples are the National Association of Women's Institute (NAWI) and the Young Women's Christian Association (YWCA). Eventually, with the presence of the more educated women leaders, imbued with the orientation of Western Liberal Feminism for women's emancipation, these voluntary associations broadened their objectives to deal with issues for the advancement of women in the economy and nation-building. Consequently, several of them grouped together and formed the National Council of Women's Organization (NCWO) in 1963, with the expressed aim to raise the status of women and to work for the welfare of children. NCWO has achieved results exemplified by the following:

1. Equal pay for men and women in the public sector.
2. Pension rights for women.
3. Better maintenance allowance for divorced women and children
4. Appointment of women to serve in the Jury and the National Council for Islamic Affairs.
5. Establishment of a Royal Commission on laws governing marriage and divorce for non-Muslims.

It can be noted that the orientation of women's organization in Malaysia has exhibited progressive developments. For instance, since 1970, NCWO has advanced to incorporate "Women in Development" issues through organizing specific committees and several conferences on the topic. The other women's organizations like the NAWI and the YWCA have also widened its focus to facilitate activities associated with the Women's Decade. Likewise the newly-formed NACIWID and the Women Affairs Secretariat have also augmented the trend fostering the "integration of women in the Development process" by playing a leading role. In the 1980s, other new women's organizations have grown. These include PUSPANITA which comprised women employees or wives of officers in the public sector and statutory bodies, and the many voluntary associations of wives of state assembly men, parliamentarians and Cabinet members which do a lot of charity and welfare work. The late 1970s and 1980s also saw the steady evolution of working women's groups like the women's section of the Malaysian Trade Union Congress (MTUC) and the Women's Aid Organization (WAO). Some leaders of these new groups provide a different ideological orientation in advancing women's status, often incorporating Women's Liberation ideology, and sometimes a clear Marxist-Feminist fervour. In addition, women's groups closely linked to various religious revivalization movements such as the Islamic Fundamentalist sects have also emerged.

Therefore, it can be said that generally, the growth and ideological orientation of the women's movement in Malaysia are very much influenced by the changing social milieu. In the early phases, the women's mass-movement was linked to the nationalist movement but essentially in the supportive gender role. Then in the

1950s and 1960s with the process of nation-building, women's voluntary associations continued to project women's emancipation mainly through Liberal-Feminist ideas. Eventually in the 1970s with the influence of the United Nations' Women's Decade, the women's movement incorporated "Women and Development" issues, and in the 1980s with the growing number of educated women in the labour force, and graduates from Western universities, the women's question is being addressed through a different ideological framework, often influenced by Western Women's Liberation and Marxist-Feminist orientation. In juxtaposition, the women's organization of the Islamic Fundamentalist movement advocates a gender model based on separate roles for men and women.

In summary, the women's movement now comprises varied and sometimes conflicting ideological leanings, thus posing the Government's Secretariat for Women Affairs, a gargantuan task in its role to coordinate and garner support from all sides for its national women's development programmes.

PART II:
WOMEN IN POLITICS

The history of women's participation in politics has been outlined in Chapter One. It was also noted in Part One that Malay women played a very active role in the quest for national independence and convinced the British colonials that they were a force to be seriously reckoned with. One such woman was Khatijah Sidek who was often involved in debates with men on the political rights of women. Another notable personality was Rahimah Abdul Rahman who toured the countryside to establish women's support for the Alliance. The wives and daughters of political leaders also provided the infrastructural support for the election such as making housecalls, etc. It was estimated that the number of Kaum Ibu members involved in the political activities was almost equivalent to the men.

A few women were present in the decision-making meetings concerning the political future of the country. Puteh Mariah, a committee member of the Kaum Ibu was one such person who was part of the working committee formed in July 1946 to consider the propositions of the Malayan Union (Zaiton Nasir, 1983: 26). However, they were not represented in the formal negotiations with the British. The monopoly by men for important positions was also noticeable when no woman was nominated to stand for the first national elections. It was only after a threat to boycott, that Halimahton Abdul Majid was nominated for the Federal Legislative Council as State-level candidate and subsequently won in the elections. In 1959, fourteen Kaum Ibu members were selected to run in the second general elections and they comprised 3.6% of the total members of electoral candidates that were fielded by the then Alliance coalition of parties (Noraini Abdullah, 1989: p. 5). Although all women above 21 years of age were given the right to vote at the same time that franchise was accorded to men, it remains a burning question why the Kaum Ibu did not voice objections to the fact that the 1957 Malaysian Constitution did not guarantee women's equality before the law. Paradoxically, it was an *Utusan Melayu* newspaper editorial which had raised some query.

Table 5.1 shows the total number of candidates who stood for and succeeded in the elections for the period 1957 to 1982. The figures indicate that there is only a slight difference in the percentage of males and females. In 1955, the percentage of males was 99.2%, while in 1982, it was 97.9%. For females, the proportion remains small, in 1955 it was 0.8% and in 1982, it rose very slightly to 2.1%. Therefore, in terms of nomination, the gender that was presented was dominantly male. However, even though the percentage of women nominated was low, it is worthwhile to note that the chances of women candidates winning in the elections were always much higher than for men.

Parliament also continues to be predominantly represented by men. However, the gap between male and female members is closing over the years. For example in 1955, the male-female ratio was 55:1 while in 1982, it was about 18:1. This indicates that generally, over the years the number of women in Parliament is increasing.

Such a trend, albeit in a smaller proportion, is reflected in the increasing number of women as full cabinet ministers, deputy ministers and Parliamentary Secretaries.[1]

Table 5.1
Candidates Who Stood For Election And Who Succeeded In 1955, 1959, 1964, 1969, 1974, 1978 And 1982 According To Sex

Year	Nominated Male	%	Female	%	Elected Male	%	Female	%	Ratio Representing M–F In Parliament
1955*	128	99.2	1	0.8	51	39.8	1	100	51:1
1959	255	98.5	4	1.5	101	39.0	3	75	33.7:1
1964	273	97.8	6	2.2	101	36.2	3	60	33.7:1
1969	366	98.8	4	1.2	142	41.8	2	50	71:1
1974	319	97.6	8	2.4	149	52.1	5	62.5	30:1
1978	391	97.5	11	2.7	147	46.7	7	63.6	21:1
1982	371	97.9	8	2.1	146	39.3	8	100	18.3:1

* Federal Legislative Election Persekutuan Tanah Melayu.
Source: Nik Safiah Karim, 1985.

Among the factors which can explain why women are still under-represented in the government, one of them would certainly relate to the system by which the political leaders are chosen in the respective ruling parties. A brief mention will be made here of the way members are selected to top positions in the Government. Although it is the prerogative of the Prime Minister to choose party members to sit as Cabinet members and in other top political positions in the ministries, this choice is often influenced by the relative strength the member has (or claims to have) in the party and in his or her own parliamentary constituency. Taking UMNO as an example, the men politicians normally would have to retain their position as head of the UMNO division in order to be seen worthy of being selected as deputy ministers or full ministers. For women politicians, historical records have shown that they should at least be representing their division as head of WANITA UMNO. So far no woman Cabinet minister has ever held the post of head of an UMNO division. In addition, women politicians are normally chosen to be full cabinet ministers if they are also head or deputy-head of WANITA UMNO. This means that they have to compete among themselves in the UMNO wing to be considered eligible for top positions in the Government. Similarly, all cabinet members, regardless of their gender, would have to show that they receive the majority support of party members as indicated by retaining their elected positions in the UMNO Supreme Council. The path up the political ladder is a competitive and complicated one. Women as well as men politicians would have to maintain their position most often—as demonstrated by history—through patronage from the "big-men" at the top as well as continual support from party members at the grass-root divisional level.

In such an environment, women party politicians can hardly afford to fight for women issues or for women organizations especially if such demands are contrary to the objectives of the party. It is also noticeable that many members of the new breed of politicians in the various political parties, men and women alike, approach politics as a career. Hence their guiding ambition is to reach the top of the career ladder. Given such aspirations, promoting an image which champions women's cause, hence representing only half of the population, may not be the acceptable one especially when these demands may alienate the men's support.

The number of women politicians at the State Legislative and Executive Councils is also increasing but as in the Cabinet they are overshadowed by men who form the majority and hold powerful portfolios.[2]

Would the future hold changes for women politicians and women's participation in politics? Can it be envisaged that women politicians will unite and represent all women's interests and welfare once they reach the top of the political ladder? The answers to these questions can only be analysed in the light of communal party politics, sectional and class interests, different ideological orientations (even among women) in a multi-racial society and a competitive environment.

Meanwhile, women continue to play their supportive role in politics, as reliable campaigners and dependable voters. It was calculated that women who registered in 1982 comprised about 50% of the total voters (Zaiton Nasir, 1982: 13). As noted by Noraini Abdullah (1989, p. 9) all things considered, Malaysian women are not simply a *residual* category, the politics of numbers and communalism have played an important part in linking women's public life to politics, what is at issue now is the *quality* of that connection, which so far has been defined by its male-dominated leadership and traditional gender ideology.

PART III:
WOMEN IN THE GOVERNMENT SECTOR

The data on women in the Government service especially in the pre-Independence period is lacking. Changes in classification and gaps in the available information also preclude the possibility of making very accurate trend statements. These limitations must be kept in mind when reading the contents of this section.

Women's work participation in the Government sector can be traced back to 1921 but they were employed mainly as low-level manual workers. Most of these women were from the Chinese and Indian immigrant groups, with very few from the Malay indigenous race. Later, with the spread of formal education for women, a small number obtained jobs in the 1940s mainly as teachers, nurses and clerical staff. This type of occupations is an extension of women's roles as supporters to men and as nurturers and carers. It was only after Independence that the number of women employees grew in the service's workforce.

However, women employees had to face several obstacles to achieve equal status with men. For example, it was not until 1964 that they were admitted into the Malayan Civil Service, now known as the Administrative and Diplomatic Service. Likewise, it was only in 1969 that equal pay was awarded and eventually in 1971, women were accorded permanent employment tenure regardless of their married status.

Obviously, the topic of women's employment in the Government service is an interesting one, not only because it is the single largest employer in Malaysia but as a Government administrative machinery, it has the challenging responsibility to convey the image of being just and fair, and a role-model as well as a reference for other employers. As discussed by Norma Mansor (1989,) the Government service is expected to take the lead regarding wages, terms and conditions of service and other matters of employment. To a certain extent, Government decisions and policies affecting its employees will have some bearing on the rest of the labour force.

The aim of the ensuing discussion however is not to analyse the terms and working conditions faced by women in the service (this information can be obtained from the references cited) but to provide an overview of the trend and pattern of their participation. Focus will be placed on two major areas, firstly, women's progress *vis-à-vis* men, and secondly, the prominent traits in women's participation pattern in the Government service.

Changing Classification Within The Service

In this chapter, Government service refers to the service that is limited to the Government sector. This excludes those belonging to statutory bodies and public enterprises.[3] In 1947, the Trusted Salary Commission of Malaya made the first classification of the occupations within the Government service according to divisional status. Under this classification, these occupations were categorized into five different categories, that is, Division I to IV, and lastly, the Industrial and Manual Group. However, the Suffian Report in 1970 later reviewed this categorization and based on functions and salary, the above five categories were reduced to four. They are as follow:

Group	Salary Scheme
Managerial and Professional	$1,250 or more
Executive and Sub-professional	$750–$1,250
Clerical and Technical Group	$250–$750
Industrial and Manual Workers	$250

But with the introduction of the Cabinet Committee Report in 1977 based on academic qualifications for direct entry, the divisions resulting from the Suffian Report in 1970 were further revised. Now, Group A consists of officers with a university degree, Group B—Diploma and Higher School Certificate, Group C—Malaysian Certificate of Education and Group D consists of employees with qualifications lower than Malaysian Certificate of Education.

Women's Increasing Participation In Gender-Based Occupations

Although men still form a very big majority in the Government service's workforce, women's participation is increasing steadily. As shown by the figures in Tables 5.2 and 5.3, women's share of the workforce is expanding while men's share is declining. For example, women's share was only 13.7% in 1957, rising to 27.0% in 1980 and 30.6% in 1987. In contrast, the men's proportion is declining from 86.3% in 1957, to 73.0% in 1980 and 69.4% in 1987.

There are several factors favouring the absorption of women employees into the Government service. Among others, these include the general expansion in Government administrative machinery associated with the implementation of national development programmes. The economic growth scenario of the 1970s and early 1980s also encouraged the Government's move to increase expenditure on job-creation and filling all job-vacancies ("Operation Isi-Penuh"). A major portion of the Government's expenditure in any rapidly developing country will be spent on health, education and welfare services, a typical pattern which has been adhered to by Malaysia. Therefore, the data show that the growth rate in women's participation increased rapidly after 1970 but was confined mainly to these service-oriented jobs. Even during the economic recession of 1982–1986, the Malaysian Government, unlike some countries of the Commonwealth, has very wisely not drastically reduced its expenditure on health and education manpower. Since women, rather than men, are favoured to fill these positions as nurses and teachers, the continual expenditure on these sectors has resulted in unstaggered absorption of women into the service's workforce. In this aspect therefore, gender-based preferences of the employer have benefited women relative to men. But that is as far as the advantage goes.

Even though women are making inroads into the Government service, it is obvious that the largest intake is in the research division and in education and health related service occupations. This is most obvious in the Division One or Group A category. As shown by the figures in Table 5.4, women are concentrated in the National Archives, Education service, Department of Inland Revenue and in Medical and Health service.

Gender-based considerations seem to remain a determining factor in labour force segmentation even in the Government service. Overall, women are still under-represented in other sectors of the service's workforce and especially in Group A posts. The percentage of women officers is small compared to men. Women officers are still a "rare species" in the Administrative and Diplomatic Service which is the elite core of government civil service and in the Telecommunications service and Public Works Department where most posts require engineering and technical training, qualifications which are generally a rarity among educated women.

Women's Participation Patterns

Focusing specifically on the structure and composition of the women's component of the workforce, it can be discerned that by 1987, the largest number are concentrated in Group C (48.5%), the second largest in Group D (35.6%) and a small number in Groups A (8.9%) and B (7.0%). (See Table 5.5). Women in Group C hold posts such as clerks, stenographers and middle-level technicians. Group D comprises manual workers and labourers. However, in terms of growth, Groups A and B have the highest rate, that is, 22.9% and 15.8% respectively as compared to Group C (9.9%) and Group D (13.2%). (See Table 5.5). Even though, statistically, this shows a very positive trend, yet it must be remembered that the growth rates are highest for Groups A and B because of their smaller starting base as compared to Groups C and D. Nonetheless, it is a favourable sign and indicates future changes in the female composition of the workforce.

Table 5.2
**Total And Percentage Number Of Staff
In The Government Sector By Sex, 1957–1967**

Sex	31.7.57	31.7.58	31.7.59	31.7.60	31.7.61	31.7.62	31.7.63	31.7.64	31.7.65	31.7.66	31.7.67[+]
Men	107,730	101,570	106,180	115,140	120,970	127,660	143,450	143,690	148,776	148,010	153,740
	(86.3)	(84.9)	(85.7)	(82.9)	(82.0)	(81.1)	(79.9)	(81.2)	(81.0)	(80.6)	(79.0)
Women	16,280	18,030	17,780	23,790	26,630	29,740	36,080	33,300	34,898	35,720	40,880
	(13.7)	(15.1)	(14.3)	(17.1)	(18.7)	(18.7)	(20.1)	(18.8)	(19.0)	(19.4)	(21.0)
Total	119,010	119,550	123,960	138,930	147,600	157,400	179,530	176,990	183,674	183,730	194,620
	(100.0)	(100.0)	(100.0)	(100.0)	(100.0)	(100.0)	(100.0)	(100.0)	(100.0)	(100.0)	(100.0)

NUMBER OF STAFF—IN PARENTHESES

* inclusive of young persons
[+] inclusive of Sabah and Sarawak
Source: Ministry of Labour and Manpower Annual Reports and Norma Mansor (1989: p. 6).

Table 5.3
Total And Pecentage Number Of Staff In The Government Sector By Sex, 1980–1987

Sex	\multicolumn{8}{c}{NUMBER OF STAFF—IN PARENTHESES}								
	31.12.80	31.12.81	31.12.82	31.12.83	31.12.84	31.12.85	31.12.86	31.12.87
Men	356,775	385,910	468,214	486,296	496,485	501,515	503,704	486,441
	(73.0)	(72.4)	(72.3)	(71.8)	(71.2)	(70.7)	(70.2)	(69.4)
Women	131,954	146,884	179,761	190,852	201,204	207,669	213,420	214,814
	(27.0)	(27.6)	(27.7)	(28.2)	(28.8)	(29.3)	(29.8)	(30.6)
Total	488,729	532,794	647,975	677,148	697,689	709,184	717,124	701,255
	(100.0)	(100.0)	(100.0)	(100.0)	(100.0)	(100.0)	(100.0)	(100.0)

Source: Central Staff Records, Public Services Department and Norma Mansor (1989: p. 8).

Table 5.4
Distribution Of Posts Occupied By Officers
In Division 1 And Group A In 1968, 1978 and 1988—In Parentheses

Services	1968 Women	1968 Men	1978 Women	1978 Men	1988 Women	1988 Men
1. Administrative & Diplomatic Service	10 (1.7)	571 (98.3)	85 (13.5)	545 (86.5)	39 (7.4)	491 (92.6)
2. Radio and Television	4 (3.1)	126 (96.9)	3 (3.3)	89 (96.7)	78 (26.6)	215 (73.4)
3. Fisheries Department	1 (4.5)	21 (95.5)	6 (10.7)	50 (89.3)	30 (17.5)	141 (82.5)
4. Department of Inland Revenue	2 (2.1)	94 (97.9)	70 (24.8)	212 (75.2)	526 (48.1)	568 (51.9)
5. Medical and Health Service	144 (17.8)	667 (82.2)	447 (19.5)	1,853 (80.5)	1,938 (36.7)	3,339 (63.3)
6. Public Works Department	2 (0.7)	285 (99.3)	22 (2.8)	771 (97.2)	180 (14.3)	1,077 (85.7)
7. Social Welfare	8 (30.8)	18 (69.2)	5 (12.5)	35 (87.5)	61 (36.5)	106 (63.5)

8. Statistics Department	4 (12.9)	27 (87.1)	14 (17.9)	64 (82.1)	52 (35.6)	94 (64.4)
9. Telecommunications Service	2 (1.7)	118 (98.3)	28 (9.4)	271 (90.6)	72 (17.6)	338 (82.4)
10. National Archives	2 (40.0)	3 (60.0)	7 (33.3)	14 (66.7)	33 (55.0)	27 (45.0)
11. Ministry of Agriculture and Co-Operative Services	1 (7.1)	13 (92.1)	2 (9.5)	19 (90.5)	42 (23.9)	134 (76.1)
12. Ministry of Defence	3 (14.3)	18 (85.7)	5 (12.5)	35 (87.5)	52 (16.1)	270 (83.9)
13. Agriculture Service	4 (4.3)	87 (95.7)	—	—	49 (18.9)	210 (71.1)
14. Education Service	50 (10.6)	420 (89.4)	1,777 (34.7)	3,338 (65.3)	9,980 (49.6)	10,146 (50.4)
15. Information Service	3 (6.5)	43 (93.5)	2 (6.1)	31 (93.9)	37 (29.8)	87 (70.2)
16. Corporation of Accountants, Malaysia	2 (10.0)	18 (91.0)	15 (15.3)	83 (84.7)	52 (32.7)	107 (67.3)

Source: 1. *List of Federal Officers, Malaysia, 1968 and 1978.*
2. *Central Staff Records, Public Service Department.*

Table 5.5
Distribution Of Women In The
Government Service Sector According To Salary Group

Salary Group	1968 No.	1968 %	1987 No.	1987 %	Growth Rate (%)
Group A	244	1.1	19,032	8.9	22.9
Group B	748	3.2	15,066	7.0	15.8
Group C	15,804	68.5	104,153	48.5	9.9
Group D	6,268	27.2	76,563	35.6	13.2
Total	23,064	100.0	214,814	100.0	

Source: Central Staff Records, Public Service Department, 1988.

Another positive development is in the professional sector of the service. More women are taking on these posts especially in the new professions. The most notable increase are among quantity surveyors, lawyers and accountants. However, most of these women professionals are concentrated in the Education and Health Services sections.

In conclusion, it can be said that despite the rapid increase of women in the Government service's workforce, their participation pattern has changed very little over the years. The "feminization" of certain jobs in the Government service continues. Women employees are also concentrated in the Group C category in occupations which reaffirmed women's secondary status as followers *vis-à-vis* men rather than as leaders. Traditional gender roles for women in the domestic domain are reconstituted in the Government service sector. Likewise, women are evidently under-represented in positions of leadership and authority. Nonetheless, entry has been made into what has hitherto been men's territory and provided that the positive trend of women's increasing participation in Group A posts, particularly in key positions of power and authority, and into various sectors of the service is sustained, there is a strong possibility that substantial changes will occur in the foreseeable future.

NOTES

[1] Under the leadership of the first Prime Minister, Tunku Abdul Rahman (1957–1969), there was only one woman minister. This number increased to two during the second Prime Minister's tenure (Tun Razak, 1969–1976) and the appointment of one woman Parliamentary Secretary. Then, during the third Prime Minister's leadership (Tun Hussein Onn, 1976–1982) there was one woman minister and five deputy ministers. With the fourth Prime Minister, (Dr. Mahathir Mohamad, 1982–) there was a total of one minister, four deputy ministers, and one Parliamentary Secretary. With the Cabinet reshuffle in 1986, there are at present two ministers and three deputy ministers.

[2] There was difficulty in obtaining data on women in the State Legislative Assembly and in the Executive Council.

[3] The Government service is the administrative machinery of the Government that plans, introduces and regulates the policies and bills that have been passed in Parliament and at the State Legislative Councils.

BIBLIOGRAPHY

Abdullah Zakaria, Adnan Hj. Nawang, Krishen Jit and Lee Kam Hing, *Malaysia: Tokoh Dulu dan Kini.* University Malaya Press, Kuala Lumpur, 1986.

Jabatan Penerangan Malaysia, Kementrian Penerangan, "Profil Pemimpin Malaysia". Jabatan Penerangan Malaysia, 1986.

Manderson, Lenore, *Women, Politics and Change. The Kaum Ibu UMNO, Malaysia, 1945–1972.* Oxford University Press, Kuala Lumpur, 1980.

Nik Safiah Karim, "Wanita Malaysia Sebelum dan Sesudah Dekad Wanita". Kertas kerja yang dibentangkan di Seminar "Dekad Wanita—Pencapaian dan Cabaran" anjuran Majlis Kebangsaan Pertubuhan-Pertubuhan Wanita (NCWO), Kuala Lumpur, Ogos 28–30, 1985.

Noraini Abdullah, "Women's Participation in the Political Development Process in Malaysia: Trends and Implications". Paper presented at the Colloquium on "Women and Development: Implications for Planning and Population Dynamics". University of Malaya, 1989.

O'Brien, Leslie N., "Four Paces Behind: Women's Work in Peninsular Malaysia", in Manderson, L. (ed.), *Women's Work and Women's Roles*. The Australian National University, Development Studies Centre, Monograph No. 32, 1983.

Zaiton Nasir, " Wanita Dalam Politik: Kualiti Bukan Kuantiti Yang Dipentingkan". *Dewan Masyarakat*, April 1982.

Zaiton Nasir, "Wanita: Kepimpinannya Belum Jelas". *Dewan Masyarakat*, March 1983.

6
The Development Of The Law And Its Impact On The Position And Status Of Women

Laws are binding rules of conduct imposed on people whereby punishments are meted out for their non-compliance. With rapid urbanization and growing complexities of civilization, people began to realize that their survival interests and those of their neighbours do not always and necessarily coincide. Their sense of right and wrong may also conflict. Thus they saw the need to lay down sets of rules to regulate behaviour and to protect individual and collective interests.

There are two sources of Malaysian laws—written laws and unwritten laws. Written laws comprise the following:

1. The Federal Constitution, that is, the supreme law of the land, and the thirteen states' constitutions;
2. Legislation enacted by Parliament and the State Assemblies; and
3. Delegated or subsidiary legislation made by persons or bodies under powers conferred on them by Acts of Parliament or enactments of State Assemblies.

Unwritten laws consist of the following:

1. English common law suitable to local circumstances;
2. Judicial decisions of Superior Courts which form the binding precedents to the lower courts; and
3. Local customs accepted as having the force of law.

DEVELOPMENT OF LAW AND ITS IMPACT ON WOMEN 125

Contrary to common belief, Law is an essential medium of change. The situation in the United States brings out this point clearly. Despite its well-known policy of liberality and democracy, the United States had some of the most discriminatory laws against women. It was not until the enactment of the Equal Rights Amendment to the Constitution in the 1970s that finally guaranteed women's rights for equality. The Equal Rights Amendment proposed to remove every last vestige of sex-based discrimination in American Law.

This chapter provides an overview of the development of certain laws in Malaysia which are of direct or specific relevance to women. It will therefore confine itself to the following areas of Law—constitutional law, labour law, income tax law, family law and rape law. In the course of the discussion, how these laws affect the position and status of women in society will also be touched upon.

AN INTRODUCTION TO THE MALAYSIAN LEGAL SYSTEM

Before the Japanese Occupation in the 1940s, the territories of Malaya had been part of the British Empire for a long time, that is, since 1786. The Straits Settlements were a Crown colony, comprising Penang, Malacca and Singapore. Other parts of mainland Malaya were the Malay Sultanates which were under the British protection. Negeri Sembilan, Pahang, Perak and Selangor formed the Federated Malay States, whereas Johore, Kedah, Kelantan, Perlis and Terengganu were Unfederated. In Northern Borneo, Sarawak was a protectorate under the domain of the white Rajah Brooke and Sabah was a colony known as British North Borneo, governed by the British North Borneo Company.

After the Japanese Occupation, there was a short period of British Military Administration in 1946. Then, the states in Malaya were reorganized into a federal state called the Malayan Union. Penang and Malacca became separate Crown colonies and, together with the nine protected Malay Sultanates, formed the Malayan Union. The British North Borneo Company parted with their rights and North Borneo was made a new Crown colony. Rajah Brooke gave up Sarawak which also became a Crown colony.

However, the Malayan Union created an uproar among the people and never got their consent. It was substituted by the constitution of the first Federation of Malaya in 1948. "Merdeka Day" on

August 31, 1957 saw the birth of the present constitution replacing the former and the Federation of Malaya became an independent sovereign headed by the Yang di-Pertuan Agong. Since then, the constitution has been amended many times. In fact, it was pointed out[1] that the constitution as it stood on August 31, 1957 is unrecognizable today.

Between 1957 and 1963, Singapore, Brunei, Sabah and Sarawak had all been moving towards self-government. But they had not abandoned their constitutional status in relation to the United Kingdom. The idea of combining all these states with the Federation of Malaya was mooted. After many months of negotiation coupled with a referendum (in Singapore), elections (in Sabah and Sarawak) and a United Nations survey, the above states joined the Federation of Malaya to form "Malaysia" on September 16, 1963.[2] Brunei, however, did not join.

In August 1965, after a series of public dispute between the Singapore state government and the federal government, Singapore left Malaysia on August 9, 1965.[3]

Since then, there has been no territorial change except internal rearrangement of carving the federal capital territory out of the state of Selangor and the federal territory of Labuan out of the state of Sabah.

The constitution, as it stands today, determines to a large extent the position, status and rights of women in Malaysia.

Generally, laws applicable within Malaysia may be divided into three categories:

1. Federal laws that apply throughout Malaysia.[4]
2. Laws that only apply to any or each of the three major components of Malaysia, that is, West Malaysia, Sabah and Sarawak;[5] and
3. Laws that apply only to any or each of the thirteen states of Malaysia.[6]

It is noteworthy that the Federal Constitution does not clearly lay down that there should be no discrimination of sex. Despite efforts to look into the possibility of inserting a more emphatic provision to that effect, nothing has been achieved so far. It will not be wrong to say that whenever discrimination of sex occurs, there is nothing to protect and safeguard the interest of women at all.

POLITICAL AND ADMINISTRATIVE RIGHTS

Since Independence in 1957, Malaysian women's rights as citizens to participate in the political and administrative aspects of the nation have been recognized and safeguarded in the Federal Constitution. This is because the relevant articles do not discriminate between male and female citizens.

Every citizen, irrespective of their sex, is entitled to vote in any elections to the House of Representatives (*Dewan Rakyat*) or the Legislative Assembly (*Dewan Negara*). Only two main conditions are imposed. They must be:

1. Twenty one years of age and above; and
2. Residents in the constituency where they vote.[7]

Women may be elected to the Senate or the House of Representatives if they have attained the age requirement, that is, 30 years old in the case of the Senate and 21 years old in the case of the House of Representatives.[8] Similar provisions can be found in the respective state constitutions whereby women may stand for election to the State Legislative Assembly.

Government posts, such as the *Jemaah Menteri* (Cabinet of Ministers),[9] Deputy Ministers,[10] Parliamentary Secretaries[11] and Political Secretaries[12] are creations of the Federal Constitution. Women are not at all prohibited from holding the above posts. In fact, women may hold political and administrative offices. They may and do take part in the running of the local Governments. They have also been appointed District Officers, Collectors of Land Revenue and Registrars of Societies.

Theoretically, there seems to be no restriction on appointing women to the posts of Chiefs or *Penghulu*. With the advent of the modern political system at all levels, the office of a *Penghulu* has been transformed from one of hereditary succession, where the father would pass it on to the son, to political appointment. Today, a *Penghulu* serves not only as head of the village but also as a judicial officer in the *Penghulu* court. This post is absorbed into the state's civil services. The selection and appointment of the *Penghulu* is made by the State Secretary although the Letter of Authority is from the *Sultan*. The *Penghulu's* authority arises from such Letter of Authority authorizing him, among other things, "to oversee the daily affairs of the villages, and to try and alleviate their problems and difficulties"[13]. Thus there is no reason that a woman cannot be appointed *Penghulu* if she is acceptable to the villagers. As a corollary, there should not be any objections to her sitting as a judge in the *Penghulu* Court, since women have already been appointed to other judicial office like Magistrates and High Court Judge, which are of higher rankings.[14]

Perhaps the only position to which women are excluded are those related to the performance of religious functions, for example, leading the congregation in prayer, a position similar to that of the *Imam;* and the solemnization of marriages as in the case of the *kathi*. There has not been much objection from the society to this state of affairs.

CITIZENSHIP AND PERMANENT RESIDENCE

The relevant provisions in the Federal Constitution regulating citizenship have caused much controversy. The various women organizations in Malaysia have been pressing hard for reform on this highly discriminative area. To say the least, there is still room for improvement.

Under the Federal Constitution, both men and women are equally competent to acquire citizenship by operation of law,[15] by registration[16] or by naturalization.[17] Apart from these provisions, Article 15 provides for the means by which wives and children of citizens can acquire citizenship by registration. There have been at least two main amendments to this important article. It is worthwhile to set out those two amendments in full to have a better picture of the development of the law and its impact on the position and status of women in Malaysia.

The original article as it stood on Merdeka Day reads as follows:

"15(1) Subject to Article 18, any woman who is married to a citizen is entitled, upon making application to the registering authority, to be registered as a citizen.

(2) Subject to Article 18, any person under the age of twenty one years whose father is a citizen or, if deceased, was a citizen at the time of his death, is entitled, upon application made to the registering authority by his parent or guardian, to be registered as a citizen if that authority is satisfied that he is ordinarily resident in the Federation and is of good character."

Article 15(1) above gives rights to the wife of a citizen to be registered as a citizen upon her application. No condition was imposed to the exercise of this right. Similar rights were given to children of a male citizen who were under twenty-one years old in Clause (2). The only conditions imposed were that he was ordinarily a resident in Malaysia and of good character. The prejudicial effect on women was that where only the mother of the child was a citizen, no such rights would be granted to the child. The generally accepted view then was that women could not transmit citizenship to their spouse or children. Only men were capable of doing that.

These two clauses were substituted by the Constitution (Amendment) Act, [18] Section 3 which came into force on October 1, 1962. These clauses read as follows:

> "15(1) Subject to Article 18, any woman who is married to a citizen is entitled, upon making application to the Federal Government, to be registered as a citizen if she satisfied the Federal Government—
>
> a. that she has resided continuously in the Federation for a period of not less than two years immediately preceding the date of the application;
> b. that she intends to reside permanently therein; and
> c. that she is of good character.
>
> (2) Subject to Article 18, the Federal Government may cause any person under the age of twenty-one years, being the child of any citizen, to be registered as a citizen upon application made to the Federal Government by his parent or guardian."

For the first time, conditions were imposed and had to be satisfied before citizenship is granted to a foreign wife. There would no longer be automatic acquisition of citizenship upon her application. She has to be of good character, and most important of all, she must have resided in the Federation for a continuous period of two years immediately preceding the date of the application and have the intention to permanently reside here.

The most welcome amendment was none other than that found in Clause (2). It enabled the child of any citizen to be registered as a citizen. Thus from 1962, the nightmare is over for women citizens as it became possible for their children to be registered as citizens as well. Its significance was that some of these children may not qualify to become citizens by operation of law, if, for example they were born outside the Federation and the father was not a citizen.[19] Clause (2) solves this problem by allowing them to be registered as citizens.

The present Article 15 was inserted by Section 25 of the Constitution (Amendment) Act,[20] in force from September 16, 1963, which reads:

> "15(1) Subject to Article 18, any married woman whose husband is a citizen is entitled, upon making application to the Federal Government, to be registered as a citizen if the marriage was subsisting and the husband a citizen at the beginning of October 1962, or if she satisfies the Federal Government—
>
> a. that she has resided in the Federation throughout the two years preceding the date of the application and intends to do so permanently; and
> b. that she is of good character.
>
> (2) Subject to Article 18, the Federal Government may cause any person under the age of twenty one years, of whose parents one at least is (or was at death) a citizen to be registered as a citizen upon application made to the Federal Government by his parent or guardian."

Some of the conditions imposed for the acquisition of citizenship by operation of law are due to the fact that Malaysians generally still hold the outdated view that women should follow their husbands and not vice versa. The same reason also prevails for not allowing foreign husbands to acquire citizenship by virtue of their marriages to Malaysian female citizens.

Article 23 clearly has its basis on this point of view. The general rule is found in Clause 1 of Article 23 which allows any citizen who has attained twenty-one years old to renounce his citizenship of the Federation. But Clause 3 of the same article expressly provides for an extension, that is, a woman even if below the age of twenty-one may renounce her citizenship in the Federation if she is married. The implication is that once a woman marries a foreigner, she may very well want to give up her Malaysian citizenship to acquire her husband's nationality. This is in accordance with the belief that a woman should follow her husband.

With the increase in the level of gender-liberation among Malaysian women, the view that women should follow their husbands is no longer acceptable. This policy should be changed. Just as in the case for men, Malaysian women should be considered perfectly capable of making their own decisions and they should be given the choice to choose whether to retain or renounce their citizenship. Their foreign husbands should also be allowed to stay with them. If the present law persists, we may see the departure of many highly educated and skilled women from the country for the simple reason that their husbands cannot stay. This will prove costly to our country's economy. Alternatively, even if there is the unfounded reluctance to grant them citizenship, they should at least be permitted to permanently reside here.

On the other hand, permanent residence has proved more and more difficult to be obtained even in the case of foreign wives. Legal recognition of this policy can be found in the case of *Meenal w/o Muniyandi*[21] which held that the wife of a citizen is not entitled, as of right, to enter and stay in the Federation. The court rejected the argument that if she was not allowed to reside in Malaysia, her right to citizenship under Article 15 would be merely illusory.

Foreign husbands suffer from an even worse position. There were instances where their Employment Passes were refused renewal even though they had been employed for more than ten years. They were not even given social visit passes. No valid reason was given for this. The time is ripe to look thoroughly into this unsatisfactory situation so as to achieve a more equitable end.

RIGHTS IN RESPECT OF EDUCATION

In Malaysia, fundamental rights to education do not exist. However, the Federal Constitution does provide for rights in respect of education in the form of Article 12. For the purpose of a more complete discussion, it is useful to set out Article 12(1). It reads as follows:

> "12(1) Without prejudice to the generality of Article 8, there shall be no discrimination against any citizen on the grounds only of religion, race, descent or place of birth—
>
> a. in the administration of any educational institution maintained by a public authority, and, in particular, the admission of pupils or students or the payment of fees; or

b. in providing out of the funds of a public authority financial aid for the maintenance or education of pupils or students in any educational institution (whether or not maintained by a public authority and whether within or outside the Federation)."

It is important to emphasize, for the interest of women, that Article 12(1) only prohibits discrimination on the grounds of religion, race, descent or place of birth. No mention is made whatsoever on sex-based discrimination. It can be argued that this is a mere omission on the part of the drafters and that men are subject to such discrimination as much as women. This argument appears to be based on very flimsy grounds. In a partriachal society like ours, the claim that men may be subject to discrimination in the field of education is unfounded. However, if a woman is subject to such discrimination, which is very likely to occur, she will have no legal recourse as Article 12 does not forbid such discrimination. It can be said that, in theory at least, Article 12 permits discrimination against women with regard to education.

Fortunately, the above interpretation is not borne out by actual practice in Malaysia. There is no policy of sexual discrimination. In fact, there are some written laws which categorically forbid discrimination against women (or men) with regard to education. One obvious example is the Universities and University College Act, 1971.[22] The constitutions of all the universities in Malaysia must adopt all the matters set out in the Schedule of that Act.[23] Section 5 of the schedule provides that:

"Subject to the provision of Article 153 of the Federal Constitution, membership of the University, whether as an officer, teacher or student, shall be open to all persons *irrespective of sex,* race, religion, nationality or class; and no test of religious belief or profession shall be adopted or imposed in order to entitle any persons to be admitted to such membership or to be awarded any degree or diploma of the University, nor shall any fellowship, scholarship, exhibition, bursary, medal, prize or other distinction or award be limited to persons of any particular race, religion, nationality or class if the cost of the same is met from the general funds of the university."

The fact that there is no policy of sexual discrimination with regard to education can further be explained by Article 8 of the Federal Constitution. Article 8(1) provides that: "All persons are equal before the law and entitled to the equal protection of the law."

The opening clause of Article 12(1) expressly includes the operation of Article 8. It may therefore be suggested that Article 12 is subject to the fundamental right to equality in Article 8. Thus, although Article 12 does not expressly prohibit sexual discrimination, such prohibition exists in Article 8, which is an overriding provision in Article 12. This prohibition on gender discrimination has always been acknowledged and faithfully followed, whether consciously or otherwise. However, it is much better if there is an unambiguous phrase in Article 12 to prohibit sex-based discrimination in respect to education.

RIGHTS RELATING TO EMPLOYMENT

At the outset, the labour laws in Malaysia do not reveal inequality or discrimination against women. These laws apply equally to both sexes although some provisions apply exclusively to women only under the guise of "protecting" women workers.

The Employment Act, 1955 (Revised 1981)[24]

This is the major legislation which regulates almost all labour relations, such as contracts of service, wages, rest days, hours of work, holidays, termination, lay-offs and retirement. There are two parts specifically applying to women only, Part VIII—"Employment of Women", and Part IX—"Maternity Protection". The Act applies to all employees who come within the definition in the First Schedule of the Act.[25]

    A. **Part II—Contracts of Service**

        This part applies to both men as well as women. The Employment Act provides for the minimum standard of terms and conditions of service so that any terms in the contracts of service which are less favourable than those prescribed by the Act will be void and the relevant provisions of the Act will prevail. They are of course entitled to provide for more favourable terms.[26]

        The Act does not prevent contracting parties from entering into terms which have not been provided for by the Act.[27] But it should not restrict the right of an employee to join a registered trade union and to participate in its activities.[28]

A contract of service for a fixed period of time exceeding one month shall be in writing.[29] Every such written contract of service shall contain a clause setting out the way by which the contract can be terminated by either party.[30] This is to ensure industrial harmony and precision so that whenever a dispute arises, the rights and obligations of either party are easily identifiable.

Either party may terminate the contract of service by giving notice of his intention to the other party.[31] The length of such notice shall be the same for both parties and shall be in accordance with the provisions in the contract of service. If the contract does not provide for such notice, the provision of the Act shall apply. The Act provides for the minimum length of notice which shall commensurate with the years of service.[32] However, the section does not prevent either party from waiving his right to a notice.

Either party may terminate the contract of service without notice by paying to the other party a sum of money as indemnity which is equal to the amount of wages which the employee would have earned during the term of the notice.[33]

A contract of service may be terminated for special reasons. The employer may dismiss, downgrade or suspend an employee on the grounds of misconduct. But this can be done only after due inquiry has been conducted.[34] On the other hand, the employee may terminate without notice if either he or his dependants are immediately threatened by danger to the person by violence or disease which he did not contract to undertake.[35]

An employer shall be deemed to have breached the contract of service if he fails to pay wages.[36] The contract of service shall be deemed to have been broken by an employee if he is absent for two consecutive days unless he has a reasonable excuse and has informed or attempted to inform the employer of the excuse.[37]

Employees on estates are to be provided with the minimum number of days' work in each month, that is, not less than 24 days. Such work should be suitable to his capacity.[38]

B. **Part III, IV, V and VI—Wages**
A substantial portion of the Act deals with wages. The Act carefully lays down provisions regarding wage period,[39] time of payment of wages,[40] payment of termination of contract,[41] lawful deductions,[42] truck system,[43] salary advances and limitations on advances.[44] The Act also stipulates that wages owed to the employees should have priority over all debts,[45] including debts secured by a charge or mortgage on property belonging to the employer.

Generally, the principle of a minimum wage has not been legally acknowledged in Malaysia. There is no provision which lays down the minimum wage that workers are entitled to receive. This could perhaps be considered as a glaring omission of the Act. However, there are exceptions. For example, between 1965 to 1972, four Wages Regulations Orders made under the Wages Councils Ordinance, 1947 were gazetted laying down the minimum wage for four categories of workers. They are:

  i. workers in the catering and hotel business;[46]
 ii. shop assistants;[47]
iii. cinema workers;[48] and
 iv. stevedores and cargo handlers.[49]

It is pertinent to note another omission which is detrimental to women workers. Nowhere in the Act is there any prohibition on employers to pay their women workers less than their male counterparts for doing the same amount of work. In other words, the principle of equal pay for equal work has not been legally recognized in this country even though the concept is by no means new, having been in existence for at least three decades. Women in the public sector are in a better position since this concept is being observed in practice. Although the private sector accepts this concept in principle, there are many instances where women workers are still subject to discrimination as regards their wages. Little or nothing can be done about it because the present law does not prohibit such a practice. Since women possess no such legal rights in the first place, legal redress is not open to them.

C. **Part VIII—Employment of Women**
Section 34 prohibits night work for female employees in the industrial or agricultural sector between the hours of ten o'clock in the evening and five o'clock in the morning. However, the proviso to the section empowers the Director-General of Labour to exempt in writing any female employees from the above restriction, subject to any condition that he may impose. Furthermore, the prohibited hours do not extend to "approved undertaking". This can be found in the Employment (Women Shift-Workers) Regulation, 1970, which reads:

> "any female employee employed in shift work in any approved undertaking which operates at least 2 shifts per day may work at such times within the hours of 10 o'clock in the evening and 5 o'clock in the morning as the Minister may approve."

As a result of that, in practice, and in the light industries sector, in particular, night-shift work for female employees has become the general rule rather than the exception. In view of this practice, the practical value of Section 34 has been called into question. Section 34 is seldom implemented or observed by the Labour Department. Since the country is undergoing rapid industrialization, the prohibition against night work is now considered uneconomical. Today, women join the labour force in ever-increasing numbers. For example, the participation of women in the labour force is almost equal to that of men in the age group of 25–54 years.[50] To prohibit women from working at night or "night-work" unconditionally can be considered impractical to the country's economic growth. Section 5 provides that:

> "No female employee shall be employed in any underground-working".

By this section, women are effectively prevented from working in underground mines and caves. Apparently, the Legislature considers underground working dangerous and unsuitable for women and Section 35 is designed to protect women from such unnecessary hazard.

On the surface, it appears that the above prohibitions preventing "night-work" and "working underground" for women have been imposed with the well-being and safety of women workers at heart. But the crucial question is whether it is prudent to employ such a blanket statutory prohibition in the name of protecting the welfare of women workers? Longer hours of operation is increasingly becoming a norm, especially in the industrial sector. Keeping this in mind, the restriction laid down in Section 34 need not necessarily safeguard and promote the interest of women. To illustrate this point, if a particular job specification essentially involves "night-work", women will be automatically excluded from taking part in such jobs. Moreover, there is no valid reason to forbid women from working during those night-shifts if they themselves choose to do so and sufficient support facilities for their welfare are provided.

Some, including the International Labour Conventions, are of the view that special protective measures, such as those laid down in Sections 34 and 35, are not exactly enacted to protect women in the first place, but rather to protect the interest of men by retaining the segmented nature of the labour market. Margaret Thornton,[51] who sympathizes with this viewpoint, presents the alarming observation made by a 1975 International Labour Organization (ILO) committee that ILO Conventions banning night-work and underground work for women were adopted almost immediately after the First World War and Second World War, or during the 1930s Depression when job offers were scarce. Paradoxically, one cannot find any corresponding attempt to "protect" women in occupations where they pose no threat to men, such as cleaning and nursing. Night-work or night-shifts were never regarded as hazardous to women in these occupations and no one has attempted to legislate against them.

Instead of being merely symbolic about their concern for the welfare of women workers, perhaps a fairer and more prudent solution would be for the Legislature to provide control and regulation with respect to employment of women at night. There should be more incentives to encourage employers to provide suitable facilities such as transport and housing to women who choose to work on night-shifts. These measures will not only safeguard the safety and welfare of women workers, but also allow them to actively participate in the process of nation-building.

It is useful to note the suggestion raised by the Federation of Women Lawyers in a paper[52] presented at the "Women and Law" Seminar organized jointly by the Law Society of Asia and the Malaysian Bar Council. They called for a joint-venture arrangement between the Government and employers in the private sector whereby both parties will make capital contributions towards the building of low-cost flats or quarters on industrial sites for the needs of female employees. The land and fixtures like the flats or quarters will remain the property of the Government whereas the cost of maintenance of such housing facilities will be borne by the private sector employers. The availability of such facilities will serve as additional incentives for workers as well as being a social benefit to them. Women workers will also be able to take an active part in night-work.

The above "protective" approach was adopted by the Legislature in the Children and Young Persons (Employment) Act No. 40/66 which regulates the conditions of employment of children.

Despite the blanket prohibition in Sections 34 and 35, Section 36, however, confers a discretion on the Minister to prohibit or permit the employment of female employees by order in circumstances or under conditions which the order may lay down. At least two interpretations can be made from Section 36. On the first interpretation, the effect of this section is two-fold. Firstly, the Minister may allow female employees to work night-shifts. This power given to the Minister is so wide that it renders the proviso to Section

34(1) redundant. Secondly, the Minister may even permit a woman to work underground *vis-à-vis* Section 35.

On the second interpretation, which is more significant, is that the Minister is entitled to prohibit the employment of women in certain circumstances as described in the prohibition order. Theoretically, the Minister can prohibit the employment of women as and when he wishes. Whether this power will be exercised to prohibit the employment of women in the event of unemployment among men is left to be seen. The law does not prohibit such a move.

D. **Part IX—Maternity Protection**
According to Section 37(1), a female employee is entitled to a minimum of 60 consecutive days of maternity leave and maternity allowance during the eligible period. Women in Government service and in statutory bodies are relatively at a disadvantage as they are entitled to a maternity leave of only 42 days.

A female employee shall not be entitled to maternity allowance if at the time of her confinement, she has five or more surviving children.[53] The amendment to this provision was brought about in 1984.[54] Previously, the limitation had been for three children only.

The proviso to Section 37(2) is important as it stipulates that where an employee is employed on a monthly rate of pay, she will be deemed to have received her maternity allowance if she continues to receive her salary during her confinement. No further maternity allowance will be due to her.

With respect to maternity protection, one should examine the recommendation by the International Labour Organization (ILO) as early as 1919 whereby they recommended that maternity leave of 12 weeks should be allowed.[55] The Convention came into force on June 3, 1921. A nursing mother was further allowed 30 minutes' break twice a day by Article 3(d). 1952 saw the enhancement of these provisions[56] to a minimum of 12 weeks maternity leave and "compulsory leave" of "no less than six weeks". With ILO's Maternity Protection Recommendation, 1952

Act 1-2, the leave was extended to a total period of 14 weeks. Other additional benefits were included such as cash maternity benefits, maternity services at home or in hospital, nursing allowance and nursing care and services to be given by competent persons. Facilities for nursing mothers including nursing breaks of one and a half hours during a working day, nursing or day care centres which are to be provided by employers and the Government or by compulsory social insurance.[57] In the public's interest, the maternity functions of women and the health of infants should be safeguarded. The Government is urged to incorporate the above provisions into the Employment Act.

Section 43 provides that a female employee cannot relinquish her rights under this part of the Act. Any conditions in a contract of service whereby she relinquishes her rights will be void and the relevant provisions in the Act will be substituted.

Ironically, the above statutory "protection" for women may lead to adverse and undesirable consequences for women. For example, before the amendment in 1984, most estates and plantations did not normally employ women with less than three children as they were entitled to maternity leave and allowance.[58]

E. **Part XI—Domestic Servants**

Section 57 stipulates that a contract to employ a domestic servant may be terminated by either party by giving 14 days' notice to the other, or where there is no notice, the payment of an indemnity equivalent to the payment of 14 days' wages must be made to the other party. Proviso to the section dispenses with the giving of notice as well as the payment of indemnity if the other party has breached the terms or conditions of the contract.

The implication here is that the law assumes that the relationship between an employer and a domestic servant is governed by a formal contract of service. The assumption is further strengthened by Section 10 which provides that a contract of service for a specific period of time exceeding one month shall be in writing. However, in practice, contracts of service for the employment of domestic servants are rarely formal or in writing. Most of the domestic servants are poor and ignorant of their rights under the law. They are not in a position to bargain with their employers at all. Even though the law assumes that the relations are regulated by a contract of service, it will be difficult to prove the terms and conditions if they are not in writing.

The Employment Act does not provide for domestic servants as extensively as it does for other workers. By the first schedule of the Act, Clause 2(5), the following provisions of the Act are not applicable to domestic servants, they are Sections 12, 14, 16, 22, 61 and 64, and Parts IX, XII and XIIA. It means that, in the case of a woman domestic servant, Part IX which concerns maternity protection does not apply. This amounts to unreasonably depriving domestic servants, the majority of whom are women, of their rights under the Act. It is difficult to see the rationale behind the specific exclusion of domestic servants from the protection of the above provisions.

The exclusion of other provisions such as Section 61 and 64 pertaining to the keeping of registers of employees or even Part XIIA concerning termination, lay-off and retirement benefits is understandable as they clearly have no application to domestic servants. However, there is no reason to take away fundamental rights of workers such as maternity protection, rest hours, holidays and annual leave from domestic servants. Of course, a domestic servant is at liberty to insist on the inclusion of the above provisions in her contract of service. The flaw of this statement lies in the fact that a domestic servant normally does not possess much bargaining power as against her employer. In the absence of any written contract, she cannot even complain to the Labour Department if her rights are infringed.

It is time to amend Schedule 1 of the Act making Parts IX and XII applicable to domestic servants.

F. **Part XII—Rest days, Hours of Work, Holidays and Other Conditions of Service**
Section 59(1) provides that every employee shall have one whole day as a rest day in each week by the employer. In the case of an employee engaged in shift work, any continuous

period of not less than thirty hours shall constitute a rest day.[59]

Section 60A(1) deals with the hours of work. An employee shall not be required to work:

i. More than 5 consecutive hours without a break of not less than 30 minutes;
ii. More than 8 hours in a day;
iii. In excess of a spread over period of 10 hours in one day;[60]
iv. More than 48 hours in a week.

However, an employee can choose to work overtime whereby she will be paid at a rate not less than one and a half times her hourly rate of pay.[61]

By Section 60D(1), every employee shall be entitled to ten paid gazetted public holidays. She is also entitled to paid annual leave under Section 60E(1). The length of such annual leave is in direct proportion to the number of years of service.[62]

An employee is also entitled to paid sick leave under Section 60F(1). Where no hospitalization is necessary, the length of sick leave is as follows:

i. 14 days if she has been employed for less than two years;
ii. 18 days if she has been employed for two years or more but less than five years;
iii. 21 days if she has been employed for five years or more. Where hospitalization is necessary, she is entitled to a maximum of 60 days' paid leave.

G. **Part XIIA—Termination, Lay-off and Retirement Benefits**
Rules regarding termination and lay-off benefits are dealt with under regulations made under the Act, namely the Employment (Termination and Lay-Off Benefits) Regulations, 1980.

Regulation 6(1) provides for the minimum amount of termination and lay-off benefits payment to which an employee is entitled:

i. 10 days' wages for every year of employment if she has been employed for less than two years;
ii. 15 days' wages for every year of employment if she has been employed for two years or more but less than five years;
iii. 20 days' wages for every year of employment if she has been employed for five years or more.

The above regulations, which apply equally to both men and women, have been criticized for prescribing payments which are unrealistically low. In times of recession, workers take a long time after retrenchment to gain alternative employment and the payments under the regulations will not even last them a month. Perhaps a fairer and more realistic rate of payment for workers in the Industrial and Manual Group and those earning less than M$500 a month would be between 20 to 40 days' wages in direct relation to the length of continuous service to replace the 10, 15 and 20 days as presently stipulated.

Employee's Provident Fund Ordinance, 1951

This law involves compulsory savings to help employees or their dependents financially at their retirement, death or disability when their normal flow of income is suddenly terminated. Employers are required to contribute a minimum of 11 per cent whereas employees contribute 9 per cent of their pay.

Workmen's Compensation Act, 1952

This is an Act to provide for the payment of compensation to workmen for injury suffered in the course of their employment. It applies to:

1. All manual workers, irrespective of income, who are not covered by SOCSO;
2. Workers in any company which employs less than five workers;
3. Non-manual workers in the private sector earning less than five hundred ringgit a month; and
4. Non-manual workers in the public sector earning less than four hundred ringgit a month.

Section 8 sets out a comprehensive list of the amount of compensation which an affected employee or the dependants of a deceased employee are entitled to receive.

Workmen who are injured can choose whether he wants to receive compensation under the Act or to file a suit in court for damages in respect of that injury. But they cannot make a claim in both tribunals.[63] Normally, the damages recoverable from the court far exceeds those provided for under the Act. If the employee fails to claim from her employer in court, she can always fall back on the Act. The only disadvantage of pursuing a claim in court is that the case will drag on for an inordinate long period of time.

Domestic servants, the majority of whom are women, are again at the losing end as this Act does not apply to them.[64.]

Trade Union Act, 1959

This is an Act relating to trade unions. It governs the powers of trade unions, trade unionists, union members and the Registrar of Trade Union. It regulates matters like registration of trade unions, rights and liabilities of trade unions, their constitution, union disputes, usage of funds, formation of trade unions, etc.

Children And Young Persons (Employment) Act, 1966

This is an Act to regulate the employment of children and young persons. It provides for the types of work which a child or young person may be engaged in, for example, light work and work that is not hazardous to their life and health.[65] They cannot be engaged in any employment for more than six days in seven consecutive days.[66] It also lays down their hours of work.

The Act is inadequate in some areas. For example, Section 13 provides that any child or young person shall be competent to enter into a contract of service. Does it mean that they will be bound by the contract even though the terms and conditions are unfavourable to them? It is also difficult to understand why the Act only applies to West Malaysia. As such, Sabah and Sarawak cannot avail themselves of the Act.

There is a peculiar and curious absence of provisions for seventeen year-olds. Section 9(1) defines a "child" as one who has not completed her 14 years of age and "young person" as any person who is not a child and has not completed her 16 years of age. Seventeen-year-olds are still minors by the Age of Majority Act, 1972[67] but the protections afforded under the Act are not applicable to them.

Finally, similar to the Employment Act, this Act does not prescribe any minimum wage for their employment.

Workers' Minimum Standard of Housing Act, 1966

This Act lays down the minimum standards for workers' housing provided by employers which are situated outside the limits of a Municipality, a Town Board or a Local Authority. This Act concentrates more on workers' housing in plantation estates. It also regulates the nurseries to be provided for infant dependants of workers whilst their parents or guardians are away at work.

Industrial Relations Act, 1967

This is "an Act to provide for the regulation of the relations between employers and workmen and their trade unions and the prevention and settlement of any differences or disputes arising from their relationship and generally to deal with trade disputes and matters arising therefrom".[68] It comprises provisions regulating recognition of trade unions, collective bargaining, conciliation, trade disputes, unfair dismissals, strikes, lock-outs, etc.

Factories and Machinery Act, 1967

This Act provides for the protection of workers from the hazards of industrial work, including occupational diseases. Working environment must comply with the minimum statutory standards, which is reasonably healthy and safe.

Employees' Social Security Act (SOCSO), 1969

This Act is the most important law in Malaysia as far as social insurance is concerned. It provides for pension payment and compensation to employees in cases of invalidity and employment injury, including occupational diseases. It applies to all industries other than those employing less than five persons.[69] Employees not covered by Workmen's Compensation Act must come under SOCSO. SOCSO covers all employees earning M$1,000 or less a month.[70]

A list of the rates of compensation is set out in the Second Schedule. Apart from that, SOCSO provides the following benefits to employees or to their dependants namely:

1. Invalidity Pension or Invalidity Grant;
2. Disablement Benefit;
3. Dependants Benefit;
4. Funeral Benefit;
5. Constant Attendance Allowance; and
6. Medical Benefit.[71]

This Act is the subject of major criticisms from almost all quarters. The main defect of this Act is the unbelievably low rate of compensation it provides for disabled workers or their dependants who died from injury sustained from accidents at work. Its miserly payment is well-illustrated by a report from the Consumer Association of Penang (CAP) in their monthly publication, *Utusan Konsumer,* of July 1982 that only 10 per cent of all the funds paid to SOCSO goes back as cash and medical benefits to employees. Surely the scheme is capable to provide much more than the present rate of compensation, even ten-fold the amount that it is presently paying out. This criticism is not new to those who are well-versed in labour law in the country but so far, nothing has been done to improve it. At the present rate, it will not be unfair to say that it defeats the whole objective of the Act which is to look after workers' interest by providing an alternative to filing a suit in the court of law in the event when they are unable to work as a result of physical injury sustained at work.

Another very disturbing feature of the Act lies in Sections 31 and 42, the combined effect of which is to forbid an injured worker from suing his employer in court to recover damages for work injury. If an employee comes under SOCSO she has to accept compensation provided by SOCSO and she cannot pursue the matter anymore in court against her employer even though the payment under SOCSO is unfair and disproportionate to the injury she sustained. These provisions in fact relieve the employer of his liabilities under the common law rather than protect the weaker section of the society. It is illogical that the weaker section of the employees who make an additional contribution from their wages, should lose all other benefits available under the law.

According to Section 20B, a widower of an insured person will be entitled to survivors' pension only if he does not have adequate means of support and if he is wholly or mainly dependant on the earnings of the insured person at the time of her death. Similar conditions are laid down in Section 27 with regard to widower's entitlement to dependants' benefit.

It is not immediately known why there is a difference between a widow's and a widower's rights to those benefits. Whereas a widow is perfectly entitled to those benefits if she remains unmarried, a widower is subject to more stringent conditions before his rights to those benefits arise. If a woman employee is to be treated equally, she should be able to confer the same benefits on her survivors just like her male counterparts.

Pensions Act, 1980 (Act 227)

Section 14 of the Pensions Act provides that where a pensionable officer dies in service, persons prescribed in the Regulation may be granted a derivative pension of not less than one fifth of the deceased officer's last drawn salary. A list of persons who are entitled to such derivative pension is found in Regulation 15(1) of the Pensions Regulation 1980:[72]

"A derivative pension or a derivative retiring allowance may be granted to —

a. the widow, the child or the widow and the child where the deceased officer is a man; or
b. the child where the deceased officer is a woman and also to the dependant widower who is permanently incapacitated, whether mentally or physically, and incapable of supporting himself at the time of death of the woman officer."

The Regulation raises a question as to why the husband of a woman officer should not be entitled to a derivative pension in the same way as the wife of a man officer? The present Regulation only grants a derivative pension to the husband who is permanently incapacitated. Perhaps the rationale behind this lies in the attitude of society which adheres to the rule that only a man has the legal obligation to support his wife whereas the wife has no similar obligation to support her husband. However, in reality, the wife may very well support the husband even though he is not incapacitated or incapable of supporting himself. If it is acceptable that he can be supported by the wife during her lifetime, it is not easy to understand why he should be deprived of this benefit after the death of the wife. Moreover, what if he is incapacitated and become incapable of supporting himself *not at* but *after* the death of his wife? The Regulation does not provide for such a situation.

INCOME TAX LAW

Before the Income Tax (Amendment) Act, 1975 (Act A273) came into enforcement, a wife's income is aggregated to that of the husband's[73] and the wife shall be treated as having no chargeable income.[74] With the Amendment Act in 1975, a new Section has been inserted. However, the new Section 45(4) did not go all out to provide for separate assessment for income tax purposes in all types of work. Only a wife who has her income from an employment can opt for separate assessment. A further amendment came in 1978 whereby a wife whose income derives from the exercise of a profession is also allowed to be assessed in her name.

Thus the present Section 45 provides that a wife may elect in writing that her income from employment or pension, or from the exercise of a profession as a duly qualified accountant, advocate and solicitor, architect, dentist, engineer, medical practitioner or pharmacist shall be assessed in her name and not aggregated with the total income of her husband.

However, her rights to separate assessment is restricted by the proviso to the Section, which states that if she is employed in a business which belongs, partly belongs or is controlled by the husband or by both of them, she is not entitled to separate assessment. Perhaps the rationale for such exclusion is to avoid an abuse of the system.

Apart from that, Section 45 is also restrictive in the sense that if the wife is engaged in a business or non-registrable profession, she is not entitled to separate assessment. With the increasing number of women venturing into the business world today, it is timely to call for yet another amendment to allow women to be assessed separately under these newly emerging circumstances.

A few other provisions in the Act are also adverse to women. For example, Section 47(1) allows an individual resident to deduct M$2,000 from his chargeable income as "wife relief" if the wife is living together with him. But if the wife is the one supporting the husband, there is no corresponding provision enabling her to make similar deductions.

Women are faced with the same problem again with respect to child relief. Proviso to Section 48 expressly disallows deductions for child relief in cases where the wife who is living together with the husband is assessed separately on her income. It would seem unfair to the wife who might have contributed financially towards the upbringing of the child. However, the wife can conceivably rely on Section 48(4) if she is living apart from the husband. Section 48(4) provides for instances where the parents are divorced. Then the child relief may be apportioned between the parties in the ratio of each contribution over their total contribution. Consequently, if the wife is the sole supporter of the child, she is entitled to claim the whole of the child relief.

FAMILY LAW

Laws Applicable To Non-Muslims

Historical Background

The area of law that has the most impact on women is none other than the Family Law. It is in this same area that some great developments have occurred. Family Law had been neglected for far too long. Calls for its reform were innumerable. The multi-racial background of the country had led to multiplicity of laws that were being applied at the same time. This had created laws which were complex to the highest extent as well as the inevitable conflict of laws.[75] These were followed by all the unnecessary hardship, suffered more by women than men.

The appointment of a Royal Commission for Non-Muslim Marriage and Divorce in 1971 to look into the unbearable legal position promised reform which was long overdue.[76] The Commission did not fail to live up to its expectation and the Law Reform (Marriage and Divorce) Bill was proposed in 1972 but became law only in 1976.[77] However, there was further delay as it came into effect only in March 1982.

Thus all the developments and improvements became realities only in the recent past. This delay is not immediately explicable in view of the fact that efforts to effect a reform in this complicated area were undertaken more than a decade ago. The Muslim–Non-Muslim dichotomy was also a hindrance in effecting a change in the field of Family Law. Muslim Law governs all matters relating to Muslim families.[78] Muslim Law is the subject matter of State laws,[79] which means the State's Legislature may make laws with respect to any matters concerning Muslim Law. Thus, Muslim Family Law is regulated by the states. The State's consent must be obtained before any changes to Muslim Law may be effected. Any attempts to bring about uniformity of Muslim Law throughout Malaysia have not been successful given the understandable reluctance on the part of the States to give up one of their few remaining powers. Nevertheless, eight states and the Federal Territory have so far enacted the new Muslim Family Law Enactment.

The Law Reform (Marriage and Divorce) Act, 1976

As mentioned before, the Act became law in 1976 but came into force only in 1982. However, even before it was enforced in 1982, amendment were made by the Law Reform (Marriage and Divorce) (Amendment) Act, 1980 (Act A498). Thus, the present Law Reform (Marriage and Divorce) Act is not the same as the original Bill but rather the amended version.

This Act applies to non-Muslims only and is regarded as a milestone in law reform. A few provisions are completely new and have never been heard of before in Malaysia. Section 5 effectively abolishes polygamy. A person cannot marry again during the continuance of his present marriage.

Section 10 provides that any marriage shall be void when either party is under the minimum age for marriage which is eighteen. An exception is laid down for a female who has completed her sixteenth year and has obtained a licence from the Chief Minister.

Another important aspect is regarding the registration of marriages. It provides for compulsory registration of all marriages.[80] Part IV of the Act lays down the procedures for such registration.

The Act gets round the hardship created when one party to the marriage converts to Islam while the other party does not. Previously non-Muslim wives could have no legal recourse if their husbands converted to Islam as they could not go under their own customary law nor the Muslim law.

Today, under Section 51(1), a non-Muslim can petition for divorce if her spouse has converted to Islam. By Section 51(2), the court, upon dissolving such marriage, is empowered to make orders with regard to the support, care and custody of the children as well as the maintenance of either spouse. Therefore, even though the Act does not apply to Muslims, persons converted to Islam after contracting a marriage in accordance to the Act can be ordered to maintain their spouse after the conversion. It is of no relevance according to the personal law (Islamic law) that the marriage is automatically dissolved on their conversion and the failure of their spouse to follow suit. This Act has solve the long-standing problem whereby neither the Syariah Courts nor the Civil Courts have jurisdiction to hear cases of this nature.

In respect of divorce, the Act allows divorce by mutual consent,[81] something which is alien to the English law on divorce on which our Act is based. This means of divorce however is not new to Malaysia. It was most commonly used to dissolve marriages under the customary law. It was expressly enacted in Section 7 of the Matrimonial Causes Ordinance of Sarawak[82] which this Act repeals. The Sarawak Ordinance is however more stringent because persons professing Christianity cannot avail themselves of this method of divorce. In fact the exclusion of Christians from this method of divorce was recommended by the Royal Commission for Non-Muslim Marriage and Divorce and was included in the draft Bill.[83] However, this exclusion was not enacted in the Act and thus all non-Muslims can present joint petitions for the dissolution of marriage by mutual consent.

The main ground for divorce is the irretrievable breakdown of marriage provided for under Section 53(1). The court shall, under Section 53(2), inquire into the alleged facts causing such breakdown and grant an order for dissolution if it is just and reasonable to do so. Section 54(1) lays down a list of facts and circumstances as proof of breakdown of the marriage. The court shall have regard to one or more of the following facts:

1. That the respondent has committed adultery and the petitioner finds it intolerable to live with the respondent;
2. That the respondent has behaved in such a way that the petitioner cannot reasonably be expected to live with the respondent;
3. That the respondent has deserted the petitioner for a continuous period of at least two years immediately preceding the presentation of the petition; or

4. that the parties to the marriage have lived apart for a continuous period of at least two years immediately preceding the presentation of the petition.[84]

From the above "facts" which the court may take into consideration when deciding whether to grant a dissolution or not, an element of fault on the part of the respondent must be proved. The only exception is Clause (d). The rest involve adultery, unbearable behaviour and desertion by the respondent. Therefore, in spite of an effort to abolish a finding of fault on either party so as to "enable the empty shell to be destroyed with the maximum fairness and the minimum bitterness, distress and humiliation",[85] most of the divorce cases will still have to rely on some fault on the other party which in the past would be included under the heading of cruelty.

There is a requirement of reference to a conciliatory body before petitioning for divorce. This is provided for under Section 106. This requirement forms one of the new features to Family Law. Although the idea of reconciliation is noble, doubts are cast as to its practical value. Firstly, divorce in Malaysia is normally frowned upon and parties to a marriage will file a petition for divorce only as a last resort when all other means of reconciliation by family members or relatives have been exhausted. To subject them further to a conciliatory body amounts to a waste of time apart from causing additional distress of waiting. Secondly, its aim is to encourage reconciliation but it is doubtful whether it can achieve its aim keeping in mind the variety of circumstances in which the requirement can be dispensed with.

The provision that is often neglected is Section 77(2) concerning the court's power to order maintenance of spouse. It is of common knowledge that a man may be ordered to pay maintenance to his wife. But many women are not aware that under Section 77(2), a wife can also be ordered to pay maintenance to her husband where he is incapacitated from earning a livelihood because of some mental or physical injury or ill-health and the wife has the means to support him. It should be pointed out that the husband's right is very restrictive indeed, but it is an improvement on the previous position where the husband had no right at all to be maintained by his wife. Some may object to this provision claiming that it is detrimental to a wife's interest as it adds responsibilities to her but it must be appreciated that this is an essential step towards equality. If women are to be taken seriously, they must know that equal rights also entail equal responsibilities.

In reality, when a wife wants to petition for a divorce, money is very important for at least two reasons. Firstly, the woman should take immediate step to live apart from the husband. Otherwise the husband can argue that she condoned his wrongdoing by not leaving. Secondly, despite his legal duty, in practice, it is very difficult to collect maintenance from the husband and it takes time to get a maintenance order. This is more of a sociological problem as not many women are self-supporting and they suffer most when their marriages break down.

The division of assets has also undergone tremendous improvement. Section 76(1) provides that the court has the power to order the division of matrimonial assets acquired by them during the marriage. Section 76(2) takes care of the situation whereby the assets are acquired by the sole effort of one party only, for example, where that party pays for the full cost of the assets. The provision recognizes the contribution made by the other party by way of looking after the home or caring for the family. This provision is significant as it ensures that housewives have a fair share of the assets although they may not have contributed financially to the acquisition of the assets.

The court is empowered to make an order for the custody of children under Section 88(1). Both parents have equal rights. But there is a rebuttable presumption that it is more beneficial to give custody to the mother where the child is below seven years old.[86] Section 91 further favours the mother in respect of custody of a child who is deemed to be legitimate under Section 75 (that is, when the parents' marriage is annulled). The mother shall be entitled to custody of the child in the absence of any agreement between the parties or an order of the court to the contrary.

These provisions deal only with the right to custody. The guardianship of the child is governed by the Guardianship of Infants Act, 1961.

Guardianship of Infants
1. LEGITIMATE CHILDREN

Section 5 of the Guardianship of Infants Act, 1961 (Revised—1988)[87] states that—

"the father of an infant shall be the guardian of the infant's person and property."

However, Section 6 stipulates that —

"where an infant has no father living, the mother of the infant shall be the guardian of his person and property:
Provided that the Court or a Judge may appoint some other person to be the guardian of the infant's person and property, or either of them to act jointly with the mother."

Section 10 empowers the Court to remove a guardian, whether a parent or otherwise.

Provision in Section 6 clearly undermines the mother's ability to act as a guardian and makes it necessary for her to act jointly with some other person. The Act was formulated in times when women were dependent on their husbands financially. The same does not apply to our society now. Several women nowadays discharge all functions previously undertaken by a father, a fact which is widely recognized in the majority of other Commonwealth countries and the United Kingdom (where our Act is derived from). The mother in these countries is automatically given equal rights to the guardianship of a child right from the outset. Despite calls from the Malaysian women's organizations for an amendment to this provision, the provision is here to stay in the revised version of the Act in 1988.

Nevertheless, the proviso of the Act allows the Court to make such order regarding the custody of the infant and the right of access by either parent.

In pursuing the powers under the Act, Section 11 provides that the Court shall have regard primarily to the welfare of the infant and consider the wishes of both the parents.

2. ILLEGITIMATE CHILDREN

Section 27 of the Civil Law Act, 1956 (Revised—1972), Act 67, provides that in all cases relating to the custody and control of infants, the law to be administered shall be the same as that of England, having regard to the religion and custom of the parties. Since there are no statutory provisions on the matter, the common law of England would apply. According to the English case of *R v*

Nash,[88] Jessel M.R. laid down the principle that the law gives effect to the natural rights of the mother. Thus the natural mother would have custody and all rights pertaining thereto over the rights of an illegitimate child.

Laws Applicable To Muslims
Historical Background
Legislative authority of Muslim Law rests with the state. Thus, Muslim Family Law is regulated by the individual states of Malaysia. This is done through the various state enactments for the administration of Muslim Law. The provisions on Marriage and Divorce in the various enactments were somewhat similar as they were all based on the *Hukum Syara'*. What did exist were differences in administrative procedures which not only led to diversity and complexity but also hardship and dissatisfaction.

The need for reform was answered by the drafting of a model statute which was in fact a codification of the Muslim Law combined with a few other provisions that were identical to the Law Reform (Marriage and Divorce) Act, 1976. Most states have accepted the model statutes although modifications were made by individual states when they eventually enacted their own laws. To date, eight states and the Federal Territory have the new legislations:

1. Kelantan Enactment No. 1 of 1983
2. Malacca Enactment No. 8 of 1983
3. Negeri Sembilan Enactment No. 7 of 1983
4. Islamic Family Law (Federal Territory) Act 1984, Act 303
5. Kedah Enactment No. 1 of 1984
6. Perak Enactment No. 13 of 1984
7. Selangor Enactment No. 4 of 1984
8. Penang Enactment No. 2 of 1985
9. Pahang Enactment No. 3 of 1987

No doubt, this brings about simplification of the law applicable in a particular state. But it does not result in uniformity in the laws of all the states in Malaysia. In fact, there is even greater diversity and this is in relation not just to administrative procedures (as, for example, the procedure in applying for permission for polygamous marriages) but also with regard to substantive requirements (like a minimum age for marriage).

Marriage

1. SEX OF PARTIES

Unlike the Law Reform (Marriage and Divorce) Act, 1976, the Islamic Family Law Enactments do not expressly provide that a marriage can only be solemnized if the parties are respectively male and female. However, since all the sections relating to marriage refer to either a man or a woman, it can safely be assumed that this marriage must be between a man and a woman, since according to the religion, a marriage must be between a man and a woman and no other.

2. AGE OF PARTIES

The Muslim Law does not stipulate in terms of years the age at which parties may marry. The Perak Enactment adheres to this position. But enactments in other states have laid down the minimum age requirement for marriage, that is, 16 years for women and 18 years for men. They have however allowed an exception. Persons below the minimum age who wish to marry may apply for permission to do so.

3. PROHIBITION OF MARRIAGES

A list of all prohibited relationships for marriage can be found in all the new laws. They are consanguinity (blood ties), affinity (relationship through marriage) or fosterage. Fosterage is either simply defined as a "relationship by suckling" in Kedah, or more specifically by enactments in other states as "the suckling of a baby up to sufficiency by a woman who is not its natural mother for at least five terms during the first two years of its life."

A man is also prohibited from having two wives at any one time who are related to each other by consanguinity, affinity or fosterage, such that if either of them had been a male, a marriage between them would have been illegal.

4. RELIGION OF THE PARTIES

All the new laws incorporated the provision that a Muslim woman is permitted only to marry a Muslim man. This is in accordance to the Muslim Law. The new law for Negeri Sembilan, Penang, Malacca, Kedah, Selangor and the Federal Territory provides that a Muslim man may marry other than a Muslim woman, a *Kitabiyah*. A *Kitabiyah* is defined as:

a. A woman whose ancestors were from the *Bani Ya'qub;* or
b. A Christian who follows the teachings of the early scriptures before the prophethood of the Prophet Muhammad; or
c. A Jewess whose ancestors were Jews before the prophethood of the Prophet Isa.

5. CONSENT TO MARRIAGE
   a. Consent of the parties
      Both parties to the marriage must give their consent. The enactments in Malacca, Kelantan and Kedah, however, provided an exception which allows a *wali mujbir* (the father or paternal grandfather) to marry his *anak dara* (a female person who has not been married and who has had no sexual intercourse) to anyone of his choice without her consent. However, three conditions must be satisfied first:

      - the *wali mujbir* or the prospective husband is not hostile to the woman;
      - the prospective husband is of the same social status as her; and
      - the prospective husband is in the position to pay maharmithil (*mas kahwin*).

      Even with the introduction of the above conditions, it is incomprehensible why a father can be allowed to force his daughter into marriage particularly when women are becoming more independent. Perhaps this provision is meant for women who are not self-supportive and their fathers feel the need to shift the financial burden of supporting them to someone else. Even then it is not known why her consent is irrelevant. She should always be given the choice to choose her own husband.

   b. Consent of the *wali*
      Apart from consent of the parties, consent of the *wali* of the woman must also be obtained. The *wali nasab* is related to the woman by lawful blood ties. Where there is no *wali nasab,* the *Syar'iah* Judge may give his consent as *wali Raja,* that is a *wali* authorized by the Yang di-Pertuan Agung. The enactments of the Federal Territory, Selangor, Negeri Sembilan and Penang do not provide for the situation where

there is a *wali nasab* but who refuses to give consent. Under the old law which is found in the enactments of Malacca, Pahang, Kelantan, Kedah and Perak, the *wali Raja* can be resorted to if the *wali nasab* unreasonably withholds his consent. The states that do not provide for the help of the *wali Raja* in this situation is actually restricting the woman's freedom to marry. While acknowledging the fact that to maintain harmony in the family, it is important to obtain the consent of the *wali nasab*. But what if the *wali nasab* refuses consent unreasonably? The use of the *wali Raja* who gives his consent only after full and proper inquiry is a fair compromise, balancing a *wali's* right to refuse consent with the woman's right to marry.

In practice however, very few women would resort to the use of the *wali Raja* if their *wali nasab* refused consent. Most of them would elope to other states or Thailand rather than to directly confront their fathers. This in turn raises endless problems of the validity of the "foreign" marriages and the possibility of its registration under local law.

6. MARITAL STATUS OF PARTIES
   a. Marital status of women

     A married woman may not marry any other man during the course of the marriage. If she is a *janda* (a woman who has been married and divorced after consummation of the marriage), she may remarry only after the expiry of *iddah* unless it is to the man from whom she was last divorced and only on production of a certificate of divorce or other documentary evidence that she is no longer married. The same procedures apply if the woman is a widow. If she is divorced by three *talaq*, she may not remarry her previous husband unless she has been lawfully married to another man and that marriage has been dissolved after being consummated.

   b. Marital status of men

     Under Muslim Law, a man may have a maximum of four wives. Under the new law, there is a control of polygamy by requiring that special permission be obtained from the *Kathi* before solemnizing a polygamous marriage. It is an offence to marry without such permission but the marriage itself will not be void if it has complied with all the other requirements for a valid Muslim marriage. However, such a marriage is not registrable except in Kelantan and the net effect is that a spouse to such a marriage may not be able to obtain matrimonial relief from the *Kathi's* courts elsewhere. To grant a permission for a polygamous marriage, the court must be satisfied that the man is capable of supporting all his wives and dependants, that he will treat them equally, that the proposed marriage will not cause "*darar syarie*" to the existing wife or wives and that the proposed marriage will not lower the standard of living of the wives and dependants. "*Darar syarie*" is defined as harm or danger in respect of religion, life, body, mind or property to the existing wife or wives. It is not correct to say that the wife's consent has been completely dispensed with because when applying to the *Kathi* for permission, the man must swear an affidavit which must indicate whether the existing wife has consented to the proposed marriage.

Divorce

In Muslim Law, this is treated as the most reprehensible of permitted acts. Divorce is a necessary evil for bringing to an end unhappiness by a marriage that has failed and is incapable of being saved.

a. Divorce initiated by a husband
This can be done by pronouncing a *talaq*, that is, a declaration in unequivocal terms of his repudiation of his wife. The new laws provided for a procedure that includes efforts to reconcile the parties. If there is consent from the other party to the divorce and the court is satisfied that the marriage has irretrievably broken down, the court will advise the husband to pronounce one *talaq*, which is a revocable divorce and the parties may resume cohabitation if they mutually consent to a *ruju'*.

However, if there is no consent, or where there is a chance of reconciliation, a committee comprising of a Religious Officer as Chairman and two other persons, one to act for each party will be appointed to effect a reconciliation. If it succeeds, the petition for divorce will be dismissed. If it fails, the court will advise the husband to pronounce a *talaq*. If he refuses to do so, there will be an appointment of *Hakam*. The *hakam* composed of two arbitrators. If the parties to the marriage authorize them to pronounce the *talaq*, they may do so. If they do not have such authority, the court will appoint other *hakam* who will be conferred the authority by the court to order a divorce.

b. Divorce initiated by a wife
There are three forms of divorce available to a married woman:

i. *Khul'* or *cerai tebus talaq* where the husband agrees to let his wife redeem her freedom by compensating him with an agreed sum of money. It must be pointed out that a woman can avail herself of this form of divorce only when she has an adequate and independent source of income or sufficient savings.

ii. *Ta'liq* is perhaps the easiest way for a woman to get a divorce. All the wife needs to prove is the breach of a promise made at the time of the marriage on the part of the husband. The only difficulty is in proving the breach. Women always have the difficulty of producing witnesses to support their case.

iii. *Fasakh* is an order for the dissolution of marriage on one of several possible grounds. The grounds are so many and varied that they cover almost every situation which a wife would wish to free herself from. A wife is entitled to get a *fasakh* if she is separated from her husband and can prove either:

- that the whereabouts of the husband have not been known for more than one year; or
- that the husband has been sentenced to imprisonment for three years or more.

In Islam, the husband has an important duty to maintain the wife. If he negligently or intentionally fails to perform this duty, the wife is entitled to get a *fasakh*.

Cruelty is another valid ground. Under the new laws, it not only means habitual assaults or other conduct which makes the wife's life miserable, but also includes a wide range of conduct, such as associating with women of evil repute, attempting to force the wife to lead an immoral life, disposing of her property or preventing her from exercising legal rights over it and obstructing her in the observance of religious obligations or practice. It could also be an act of cruelty if the husband has more than one wife and does not treat them equally.

Insanity of the husband for at least two years can be a ground for divorce. Another ground is that the husband is suffering from a venereal disease in communicable form.

Lack of consent to the marriage entitles the wife to get a *fasakh* in two circumstances:

i. Where the *wali mujbir* has given a girl in marriage before the age of sixteen and she repudiates it before the age of eighteen, the marriage not having been consummated; and
ii. Where the woman did not consent to the marriage or her consent was not valid, like when it was obtained by duress, mistake, unsoundness of mind, or any other vitiating circumstances recognized by *Hukum Syara'*.

Dissolution Of Marriages By Conversion

All the new laws provide that the conversion, whether into Islam by a party to a non-Muslim marriage or out of Islam by a party to a Muslim marriage, will not operate to dissolve the marriage until and unless confirmed by the court. There will be no "automatic" divorce as such. This is in accordance to the decision by the English Court of Appeal in the case of *Viswalingam v Viswalingam*.[89]

Guardianship And Custody Of Infants

Hadhanah means the caring of young children, providing for their welfare, protecting them from harm and educating them so that they will develop physically, mentally and spiritually, to become independent and able to face life and shoulder responsibilities.

The welfare of the child is the child's fundamental right. The purpose of *hadhanah* is to look after this right and it should be given preference to the right of those who claim the right of custody.

The *hadhinah* is the woman who is responsible for the upbringing of the child. A wife who has been divorced has a better right to look after the child but the father retains the right of guardianship. The father also has the right to visit and be with the child.

No remuneration shall be due to the mother for *hadhanah* as long as she is married to the child's father or during her period of *iddah* after the divorce. After that period, she is entitled to remuneration if she is nursing the child.

LAWS RELATING TO SEXUAL OFFENCES

Despite the insensitivity shown by some of our male Members of Parliament during the parliamentary debates in 1989 on the amendments to the Penal Code, the Criminal Procedure Code and the Evidence Act, 1950, relating to sexual offences, the amendments undoubtedly improve women's position and rights in this area tremendously.

One of the important changes is in raising the age limit of statutory rape in Section 375 from 14 years to 16 years. When a man has sexual intercourse with a girl below 16 years, he commits rape. It is no defence that the girl consents or even actually invites or provokes him. The court will also not consider the girl's behaviour or appearance as a mitigating or exonerating factor.

Another amendment is in Section 354 which concerns assault or use of criminal force to a person with intent to outrage that person's modesty. Under the old law, the punishment was imprisonment, extending to two years or fine or whipping or with any two of such punishment. In 1989, the maximum punishment is 10 years, fine and (or) whipping as before. At this juncture, it is important to note that there will be no outrage of a woman's modesty if she consents to it.

Perhaps the most important change lies in the prohibition to refer to past sexual history or the present sexual activities of the complainant. This is to recognize a woman's right to her own choice of values, and occasions and men. Her general conduct in relation to sex with others should be of no relevance to the specific allegation against someone else interfering with the sanctity of her body, against her wish.

There are only three exceptions to the general rule that a woman's other sexual activities cannot be questioned in court. The first exception is questions aimed "to rebut the prosecution's evidence on the complainant's sexual activity that was previously adduced." This would appear to mean that if the complainant keeps quiet about her virtues and vices, she may not be questioned by the accused or his counsel as to her past misdeeds. The second exception is questions with a view "to establish the identity of the person who had sexual activity with the complainant on the occasion set out in the charge." The wrong person may be identified when the offence is committed while they are in a group of generally morally-loose persons.

The third exception "relates to the sexual activity which is contemporaneous and will apply only where the defendant alleges belief in consent on the basis of the sexual conduct of the complainant on the same occasion." An example would perhaps be in a situation where a girl of loose virtue agrees to have sex with three men one after another. By the time the third person's turn comes, she may be too exhausted and she would have protested. Here, the third person, that is the accused can allege belief in her consent and may ask the complainant any questions regarding her sexual activity with any person other than the accused.

It is unfortunate that the Act does not provide for any illustrations. Nevertheless, the improvement on a woman's position is clear, that there will no longer be any probing with regard to her sexual activity as in the past.

Another change is made to Section 312 of the Penal Code, that is, concerning the causing of miscarriage. It can be assumed that the effect of this amendment throws the doors of abortion wide open, leading to possible abuse.

Before the amendment, the only excusable ground to cause a woman to miscarry was that it was caused in good faith for the purpose of saving the woman's life. According to the new amendment, a medical practitioner would not have committed an offence "if such medical practitioner is of the opinion, formed in good faith, that the continuance of the pregnancy would involve risk to the life of the pregnant woman or injury to the mental or physical health of the pregnant women, greater than if the pregnancy were terminated." With this piece of legislation, a pregnancy may lawfully be terminated to secure a relatively small improvement on the woman's health. It is common knowledge that some unscrupulous doctors charge sky-high fees to perform abortions. It is unwise for the Legislature to give a blank cheque to an individual that is a doctor to determine the need for all types of abortions.

If the amendment is meant to benefit rape victims, it could easily have done so by providing in clear words to that effect.

The new amendments are more of a deterrent nature. While not denying the importance of laws that deter the commitment of crimes, in this aspect, it is equally important that the victims are willing to make police reports immediately so as to assist in effective methods of investigation and detection by the police. The victims should not be subject to any harassment whatsoever. In any event, the effectiveness of this recent amendment to curb the social evil of rape is left to be seen. Hopefully, the incidence of rape will be reduced.

Perhaps other proposals should have been adopted. For example, the prohibition on probing into the past sexual history of the woman should have been extended to all sexual offences, including attempted rape and outrage of modesty. Apart from the minimum of five years mandatory imprisonment on a convicted rapist, he should also be given mandatory whipping.

CONCLUSION

It is clear from the preceding discussion that the improvements on the position and status of women via legislation are slow but forthcoming. However, once a positive improvement is made to the old legislation, it is always a big step ahead and it should improve tremendously the position and status of women. The objective is to move towards gender equality which involves equal rights as well as equal responsibilities. There are also signs of recognition of women's contribution to the well-being of the nation and its economic development.

It can be concluded that despite some limitations in certain areas of the law, it does generally cater to the interest of women as a whole. It cannot be denied that there is always room for improvement geared towards overcoming situations which promote sexual discrimination and inequality. These features may already be inherent in some laws.

Another area of improvement is by upgrading the level of legal literacy among women in the country. In fact, this is the basis for them to assert their rights and claim redress for infringements.

Therefore, there is a real and urgent need for a more effective legal literacy programme in Malaysia which extends to all areas, geographically and socially, so that women in rural and urban areas, the rich as well as the poor, can understand their legal rights and means for due protection.

NOTES

1. Tommy Thomas, "The Role of the Judiciary; the Judiciary's duty under the Constitution". Paper presented during the Aliran Conference on "Reflections on the Malaysian Constitution: 30 years after Merdeka", on August 15–16, 1987.
2. Malaysia Act, 1963, Federation of Malaya Act No. 26 of 1963.
3. The Constitution and Malaysia (Singapore Amendment) Act, 1965.
4. For example, the Law Reform (Marriage and Divorce) Act, 1976, Act 164.
5. For example:
    i. The Guardianship of Infants Act, 1961, Federation of Malaya Act No. 13 of 1961.
    ii. The Guardianship of Infants Ordinance, Sabah Ordinance No. 4 of 1946, Cap. 54, Laws of North Borneo, Revised Edition, 1953.
    iii. The Guardianship of Infants Ordinance, Sarawak Ordinance No. 23 of 1953, Cap. 93, States Laws of Sarawak, Revised Edition, 1967.
6. For example, the Islamic Family Law Enactments of the various states of Malaysia.
7. Article 119.
8. Article 47.
9. Article 43.
10. Article 43A.
11. Article 43B.
12. Article 43C.
13. Salleh Omar, "Village Politics and Traditional Dispute Resolution Methods", Project Paper, Faculty of Law, University of Malaya. 1981/82, *op. cit.*, Appendix IV, quoting a Trengganu letter of authority on February 10, 1970.

[14] Subordinate Courts Act, 1948 (Act 92) gives local *Penghulu* in Peninsular Malaysia civil jurisdiction in minor suits, where the subject matter is not more than M$50, where all parties to the proceedings are "persons of an Asian race speaking and understanding the Malay language"; and a criminal jurisdiction, restricted to a maximum fine of M$25, is exercised over "persons of an Asian race."

[15] Article 14.
[16] Article 16 and 16A.
[17] Article 19.
[18] Act 14/1962.
[19] Federal Constitution, Second Schedule.
[20] Act 26/1963.
[21] (1980) 2 M.L.J. 299.
[22] Act 30.
[23] Section 8(1)
[24] Act 265
[25] First Schedule, Section 2(1): Employee means—

FIRST SCHEDULE
[Section 2(1)]

Employee	Provision of the Act not applicable
1. Any person, irrespective of his occupation, who has entered into a contract of service with an employer under which such person's wages do not exceed one thousand ringgit a month.	
2. Any person who, irrespective of the amount of wages he earns in a month, has entered into a contract or service with an employer in pursuance of which—	
i. he is engaged in manual labour including such labour as an artisan or apprentice:	

Provided that where a person is employed by one employer partly in manual labour and partly in some other capacity such person shall not be deemed to be performing manual labour unless the time during which he is required to perform manual labour in any one wage period exceeds one-half of the total time during which he is required to work in such wage period;

ii. he is engaged in the operation or maintenance of any mechanically propelled vehicle operated or goods or for reward or for commercial purposes;

iii. he supervises or oversees other employees engaged in manual labour employed by the same employer in and throughout the performance of their work;

iv. he is engaged in any capacity in any vessel registered in Malaysia; or

v. he is engaged as a domestic servant.

Sections 12, 14, 16, 22, 61 and 64 and Parts IX, XII and XIIA.

[26] Section 7.
[27] Section 7B.
[28] Section 8.
[29] Section 10(1)
[30] Section 10(2).
[31] Section 12(1).
[32] Section 12(2):

a. 4 weeks' notice if the employee has been employed for less than 2 years.
b. 6 weeks' notice if the employee has been employed for 2 years or more but less than 5 years.
c. 8 weeks' notice if the employee has been employed for 5 years or more.

[33] Section 13(1).
[34] Section 14(1).
[35] Section 14(3).
[36] Section 15(1).
[37] Section 15(2).
[38] Section 16(1).
[39] Section 18.
[40] Section 19.
[41] Sections 20 and 21.
[42] Part IV, Section 24
[43] Part V.
[44] Section 22.
[45] Section 31.
[46] Wages Council Order.
[47] Wages Regulations (Shop Assistance) Order, 1970.
[48] Wages Regulations Order, 1972.
[49] Wages Regulations Order, 1977.
[50] Noor Farida Ariffin, "Legal Protection for Women Workers Within and Outside the Home."
[51] Thornton, M., "Job Segregation, Industrialization and Non-Discrimination Principle". Paper presented at the "3rd Women and Labour Conference", Adelaide, 1982.
[52] "Women and Employment in Malaysia", April 1983.
[53] Section 37(1)(c).
[54] Employment (Amendment) Act, 1984, Act A610.
[55] ILO Convention No. 3.
[56] ILO Convention No. 103: Article 8(2)–(3).
[57] ILO: Maternity Protection Recommendation, 1952, Article 3.
[58] Noor Farida Ariffin, "Legal Protection for Women Workers Within and Outside the Home", 1984.
[59] Section 59(1A).
[60] Section 60A(1B)* "spread over period of work" means a continuous period reckoned from the time the employee

commences work for the day up to the time that he ceases work for that day, inclusive of any period or periods of leisure, rest or break within such continuous period.

[61] Section 60A(3) (a).

[62] Section 60E(1):

    a. 8 days a year if she has been employed for less than two years.
    b. 12 days a year if she has been employed for 2 years or more but less than 5 years.
    c. 16 days a year if she has been employed for 5 years or more.

[63] Section 41(1).

[64] Section 2(1)(c).

[65] Section 2.

[66] Section 4.

[67] Act 21, Section 2 provides that a person attains the age of majority at the age of 18.

[68] Preamble to the Industrial Relations Act, 1967.

[69] Section 3(1).

[70] Section 2(5), First Schedule.

[71] Dunston Ayadurai, "The Employer, the Employee and the Law in Malaysia", 1985, page 246.

[72] Published as P.U.(a) 176/80 and amended by Act A568/83.

[73] Section 45(2).

[74] Section 45(3).

[75] For example, in 1957, there were in force, Customary Family Laws of the Hindu and Chinese, Muslim Law and four statutes regulating marriage and divorce. In 1963, the list was expanded to include Customary Laws of the indigenous tribes of Sabah and Sarawak in addition to six statutes regulating marriage and divorce. The most obvious conflict arose in cases where non-Muslim converted to embrace Islam and then marry again under the Muslim Law when the former marriage has not been dissolved.

[76] Customary laws were uncertain in some aspects. Some of them were also prejudicial as against women. For example, Chinese women cannot get a divorce under the Chinese Customary Laws unless their husbands agree to the divorce.

[77] Act 164.

[78] Ninth Schedule, List II, Federal Constitution.

[79] Article 74(2), Federal Constitution.

170 WOMEN AND DEVELOPMENT IN MALAYSIA

[80] Sections 25–27, 31 and 35.
[81] Section 32.
[82] Cap. 94, Laws of Sarawak.
[83] Clause 49, Law Reform (Marriage and Divorce) Bill, 1972.
[84] Section 54(1).
[85] Law Commission Report: Reform of the Grounds of Divorce. The Field of Choice, para 15 (mnd 3,123).
[86] Section 88(3).
[87] Act 351.
[88] 10 Q.B.D. 454.
[89] (1980) 1 M.L.J. 10.

7

Underlying Issues For Further Consideration

The "Women's Question" in development is definitely the common thread underlying all chapters of this book. Has the development process improved their position in society or downgraded their status? Has it in fact widened the gender gap? Does economic advancement of women necessarily mean that there is a commensurate trend towards gender equality? To attempt to answer all these questions would require writing another book. In summing up, it can be said that the consequences of the development process for women in Malaysia—as elsewhere—are multi-faceted and complex because although women as a group of people share a *common sex*, but in social reality they are a differentiated lot owing to differences such as social class position, ethnicity, physical appearance, residential location, different chronological and cohort point of entry into the development process, and extent of incorporation into the development scenario as well as due to socially-different designated status simply by being labelled as "married women", "spinsters", or "widows". Due to these differences, their *gender* experience will also differ and the effects of the development process on each of these different groups of women will also differ. Some groups of women gained while others remained marginalized. While taking note of this qualifier to what hitherto has been a blanket approach to "women in development" as similarly displayed in this book, the rationale for such an approach is due to the objective of providing an introductory and preliminary analysis on women and development in Malaysia. A more detailed analysis which takes into consideration the qualifier mentioned above is definitely required.

INDICATORS OF WOMEN'S POSITIVE PARTICIPATION AND STATUS

Although the approach taken in this book is to validate the authors's assertions about women's participation with supportive "hard" statistical data, yet it must not be overlooked that "soft" qualitative analyses are equally important, if not more essential. Much of the central issues on the consequences of the development process for women's status go far beyond the ambit of available statistics but require an insightful and empathetic appraisal of women's actual experiences, both past and present, on the basis of oral as well as the written media. This is in fact an issue touched upon in Chapter Four when assessing women's gains from the performance of the medical and health care system. As noted in this chapter, statistics about women's health position in Malaysia in relation to health and medical facilities definitely show positive gains but all these are not sufficient to reveal the areas needing further improvements. One such area of crucial relevance lies in the nature of the relationship between doctors and patients. As a heritage of the colonial medical structure, the modern medical system of Malaysia, similar to many other countries of the world, is still very much male-dominated as well as class aligned, hence the doctor-patient relationship is essentially between unequals with the doctor as the regnant of superior knowledge and judgement and the patient as a passive recipient of prescriptions. This situation is felt most acutely when inexperienced women are undergoing their first childbirth or facing menopausal problems. With the trend towards privatization of medical services and health care, there is also an urgent need to ensure that medical practitioners are not motivated more by monetary profits rather than keeping to the ethics of this noble profession. Similarly, provisions must be made for safeguarding patients' basic rights as consumers as well as educating them about recourse to compensation claims and benefits.

WHY AND HOW HAVE WOMEN BEEN INCORPORATED INTO THE NATIONAL DEVELOPMENT PROCESS?

In the Introduction to this book, the following questions were raised: Why has the women component been incorporated into the mainstream development activities? Why is it that women are now fully acknowledged as an essential agent of the national development process? Although these aspects are not analysed in detail in this book, it is confirmed by the historical evidence that it is essentially because women were instrumental to the achievement of manmade development objectives. As discussed in Chapter Five, in the arena of politics, they were instrumental to rally mass support for political goals. Women were and still are reliable political party workers, loyal voters and supporters. In a situation of an expanding economy and due to a quest to pursue growth, the national leadership although male-dominated realizes the need to optimally utilize the best available human resources and therefore cannot afford to ignore the potential contribution of their womenfolk who forms half the population. The need for continued economic advancement so essential for the survival of a young nation therefore prompts male leaders not to succumb to male-chauvinistic values in favour of a more pragmatic approach towards integrating women in mainstream development. Women in Malaysia also realizes that much of the impetus for women's present advancement has been due to men's decisions and encouragement and this partly explains for their alignment with their men leaders and their lack of acceptance of the more militant Women's Liberation approach when demanding for women's rights and integration in development. Within the cultural context of Malaysian society, Malaysian women leaders realize that more losses will be incurred and lesser gains derived when demands are made in a confrontational stance. Asian values of "face-saving" is of prime importance in any negotiation especially when the situation is the handing over of rights from a superior to a subordinate. More concrete and long-term benefits will therefore accrue to both sides from a conciliatory and friendly approach.

What are the other circumstances in present day Malaysia which facilitate the advancement of Malaysian women? Two outstanding ones are noticeable. Firstly, as members of a young progressive nation so very optimistic about "the good life" to be gained from economic development and wishing to be admitted as equal partners in the advanced world community, most Malaysian parents of this present generation do not usually practise gender discrimination on their daughters *to the extent* perceivable in other more traditional and homogeneous settings such as in Pakistan, Bangladesh, India and other South Asian countries. The early experience of gender for most of the modern women in Malaysia is therefore not as painful or as traumatic as that of their sisters in some other countries and as such this is one explanatory factor why they do not retaliate as violently against men in their quest for gender equality and a fair deal in life.

Secondly, it is the prevailing political and economic situation. The socio-cultural milieu in present day Malaysia while idealizing growth, racial tolerance and harmony, still exists in a political atmosphere of continuing inter-ethnic rivalry and competition. Paradoxically, this provides a conducive environment for women's advancement. This is because the progress and survival of each ethnic group regardless of sex is still the prime concern of many and this preoccupation renders "the battle of the sexes" a less important position in the list of strategic priorities. However unpalatable this may sound, yet this is a social reality which cannot be overlooked by social observers and political analysts. Given this scenario as outlined and which is situated in the flourishing Pacific Rim Economy characterized by growing opportunities for women, it is quite definite that any educated woman in Malaysia, who is prepared to make full use of the situation and daring enough to discard gender inhibitions, can rise in almost any profession that she chooses.[1]

All of the above are, of course, submissions to be tested for their validity and may be utilized as hypotheses for further research and deliberation.

NOTES

[1] This is particularly so with the rapidly expanding opportunities for women in the Pacific Rim countries as explained by Naisbitt, J. and Aburdene S. in *Megatrends 2000, Avon Press, 1989.*

Bibliography

Abdullah Zakaria, Adnan Hj. Nawang, Krishen Jit and Lee Kam Hing. *Malaysia: Tokoh Dulu dan Kini.* University Malaya Press, Kuala Lumpur, 1986.

Annuar Ali, "Industrial Restructuring: Beyond the Industrial Master Plan". Paper presented at the MIER 1988 National Outlook Conference, November 1988.

Byrne, Eileen M., *Women and Education.* Tavistock Publications Ltd., Great Britain, 1978.

Chia, Siow Yue, "Women's economic participation in Malaysia", adapted from *Women's Economic Participation in Asia and the Pacific,* United Nations, Economic and Social Commission for Asia and the Pacific, 1987.

Chee, Heng Leng, *The Development of Health Care Systems in Malaysia: Achievements and Shortfalls, December 1988.*

Department of Statistics, Malaysia (various years), Vital Statistics.

Dunston Ayadurai, *"The Employer, the Employee and the Law in Malaysia",* Singapore, 1985.

Faridah Shahadan and Madeline Berma, "Economic Development Trends and Women's Participation in the Service Sector: A macro-level analysis of interrelationships, impact and implication on development planning, 1957–1980." Paper presented at the Colloquium on *Women and Development—Implications for Planning and Population Dynamics,* University of Malaya, January 1989. Population Studies Unit, Faculty of Economics and Administration, University of Malaya, 1990.

Hamid Arshat, et. al., *Marriage and Family in Peninsular Malaysia: Analytic report on the 1984/85 Malaysia Population and Family Survey*, Kuala Lumpur, 1988.

Jabatan Penerangan Malaysia, Kementerian Penerangan. *Profil Pemimpin Malaysia.* Jabatan Penerangan Malaysia, 1986.

Jamilah Ariffin, "The aims and methods of life-long learning (or re-education) in the context of women's participation in society and lifelong education". Unpublished paper presented at the International Conference on Women and Development, Saitama, Japan, October 1984.

Jamilah Ariffin, "Economic Development and Women in the Manufacturing Sector—A macro-level analysis and with reference to 'Women and Development' issues". Paper presented at the Colloquium on *Women and Development in Malaysia—Implications for Planning and Population Dynamics,* January 1989. Population Studies Unit, Faculty of Economics and Administration, University of Malaya, 1990.

Jamilah Ariffin (1980), "The Position of Women Workers in the Manufacturing Industries in Malaysia" in Evelyn Hong, *Malaysian Women: Problems and Issues,* CAP Publications, Penang, 1980.

Jamilah Ariffin (1984), "Impact of Modern Electronics Technology on Women Workers in Malaysia" in Aziz, Yip and Ling (eds.), *Technology, Culture and Development,* University of Malaya Press, 1984.

Jamilah Ariffin (1982), "Industrialization, Female Labour Migration and Changing Pattern of Malay Women's Labour Force Participation" in *Journal of South-East Asian Studies.*

Jayaweera, Swarna, "Class and Gender in Education and Employment". Unpublished paper, Colombo, December 1987.

Kamal Salih, "The Changing Face of the Malaysian Economy", Seminar on Business Opportunities and Entrepreneurship. Kuala Lumpur, 1987.

Kaur, Amarjit, "An Historical Analysis of Women's Economic Participation in Development". Paper presented at the Colloquium on *Women and Development—Implications for Planning and Population Dynamics,* University of Malaya, January, 1989. Population Studies Unit, Faculty of Economics and Administration, University of Malaya, 1990.

BIBLIOGRAPHY

Kaur, Manjit, "Women and Education: The Development of Women in Malaysia and Some Implications for Planning and Population Dynamics". Paper presented at the Colloquium on *Women and Development—Implications for Planning and Population Dynamics*. University of Malaya, January 1989. Population Studies Unit, Faculty of Economics and Administration, University of Malaya, 1990.

Lang, Chin Ying, "Women in Business". Paper presented at the Colloquium on *Women and Development—Implications for Planning and Population Dynamics*, University of Malaya, January 1989.

Malaysia Committee of Council of the Malaysian Medical Association, *The Future of the Health Services in Malaysia: A report of a Committee of Malaysian Medical Association*. Malaysian Medical Association, 1980.

Manderson, Lenore, *Women, Politics and Change. The Kaum Ibu UMNO, Malaysia, 1945–1972*. East Asian Social Science Monographs, Oxford University Press, Kuala Lumpur, 1980.

Manderson, Lenore (ed.), *Women's Work and Women's Role*. The Australian National University, Australia, 1983.

Masitah Mohd. Yatim, "Development Process and Malaysian Female Fertility: A Macro Analysis of Trends and Patterns, 1957–1987". Paper presented at the Colloquium on *Women and Development in Malaysia—Implications for Planning and Population Dynamics*, University of Malaya, January 1989. Population Studies Unit, Faculty of Economics and Administration, University of Malaya, 1990.

Ng, Cecelia, "Impact of Agricultural Development on Rural Women: From Producer to Housewife?" Paper presented at the Colloquium on *Women and Development—Implications for Planning and Population Dynamics*, University of Malaya, January 1989. Population Studies Unit, Faculty of Economics and Administration, University of Malaya, 1990.

Nik Safiah Karim, Dr., "Wanita Malaysia Sebelum dan Sesudah Dekad Wanita." Kertas kerja yang dibentangkan di Seminar *Dekad Wanita—Pencapaian dan Cabaran*, anjuran Majlis Kebangsaan Pertubuhan-Pertubuhan Wanita (NCWO), Kuala Lumpur, Ogos 28–30, 1985.

Noor Farida Ariffin, "Legal Protection for Women Workers Within and Outside the Home." 1984.

Noor Laily binti Abu Bakar, Datin, *et. al.*, "The Changing Ethnic Pattern of Mortality in Malaysia: 1957-1979", *National Family Planning Board Research Paper*, No. 6, February 1983.

Noraini Abdullah, "Women's Participation in the Political Development Process in Malaysia: Trends and Implications". Paper presented at the Colloquium on *Women and Development: Implications for Planning and Population Dynamics,*. University of Malaya, 1989. Population Studies Unit, Faculty of Economics and Administration, University of Malaya, 1990.

O'Brien, Leslie N., "Four Paces Behind: Women's Work in Peninsular Malaysia", in Manderson, L., (ed.) *Women's Work and Women's Roles*. The Australian National University, Development Studies Centre, Monograph No. 32, 1983.

O'Brien, Leslie N., *Class, Sex and Ethnic Stratification in West Malaysia, with particular reference to women in the profession*. Ph.D. Thesis, Monash University, Australia, 1979.

Raj Karim, Dr., "Impact of Government Medical and Health Facilities on the Status of Maternal Health in Malaysia." Paper presented at the Colloquium on *Women and Development in Malaysia—Implications for Planning and Population Dynamics*, University of Malaya, January 1989. Population Studies Unit, Faculty of Economics and Administration, University of Malaya, 1990.

Salleh Omar, "Village Politics and Traditional Dispute Resolution Methods". Project Paper, Faculty of Law, University of Malaya.

Shamsulbahriah Ku Ahmah, "Stratification and Occupational Segmentation in the Peninsular Malaysia Labour Force: A case for gender-oriented development planning". Paper presented at the Colloquium on *Women and Development—Implications for Planning and Population Dynamics*, University of Malaya, January 1989. Population Studies Unit, Faculty of Economics and Administration, University of Malaya, 1990.

Siti Rohani Yahya, "The Development Process and Women's Labour Force Participation—A macro-level analysis of patterns and trends, 1957-1987". Paper presented at the Colloquium on *Women and Development—Implications for Planning and Population Dynamics*, University of Malaya, January 1989. Population Studies Unit, Faculty of Economics and Administration, University of Malaya, 1990.

Sharifah Hapsah Shahabudin, Dr., "Women in the Medical and Health Professions". Paper presented at the Colloquium on *Women and Development in Malaysia—Implications for Planning and Population Dynamics,* January 1989. Population Studies Unit, Faculty of Economics and Administration, University of Malaya, 1990.

Tan, Poo Chang, et. al., "Sex Differentials and Mortality Trends in the Process of Development in Malaysia". Paper presented at the Colloquium on *Women and Development in Malaysia—Implications for Planning and Population Dynamics,* January 1989. Population Studies Unit, Faculty of Economics and Administration, University of Malaya, 1990.

Tan, P.C., et. al., "Socio-Economic Development and Mortality Patterns and Trends in Malaysia", *Asia Pacific Population Journal,* Volume 2, No. 1: 3–20, 1980.

Thomas, Tommy, "The Role of the Judiciary; the judiciary's duty under the constitution". Paper presented during the Aliran Conference on "Reflection on the Malaysian Constitution: 30 years after Merdeka", August 15–16, 1987.

Thornton, Margaret, "Job Segregation, Industrialization and Non-Discrimination Principle". Paper presented at the Third Women and Labour Conference, Adelaide, 1982.

Zaiton Nasir, "Wanita Dalam Politik: Kualiti Bukan Kuantiti Yang Dipentingkan". *Dewan Masyarakat,* April 1982.

Zaiton Nasir, "Wanita: Kepimpinannya Belum Jelas". *Dewan Masyarakat,* March 1983.

INDEX

Abdullah Zakaria, 122, 175
Aborigines, 2
Abortion, 75
Aburdene, S., 174
Acheh, 5
Adat, See Customary laws.
Adat Perpateh, 3
Adat Temenggong, 3
Adnan Hj. Awang, 122, 175
Age-specific death rate by ethnic group in Peninsular Malaysia, 1984–1986,
    for females, 80
    for males, 79
Agricultural mechanization, 41
Ahmad Lufti, 16
AIM, *See* Asian Institute of Management.
Aliens Ordinance, 1933, 13–14
Anak dara, 157
Angkatan Wanita Sedar, 9, 106
Annuar Ali, 51, 175
Arabia, 2
Aristocratic women, 3
Aristocrats, 2
ASEAN-Australia Project, 69
Asean countries,
    Indonesia, 86–87
    Malaysia, 18, 86–88, 126
    Philippines, 86–87
    Singapore, 86–88
    Thailand, 86–87
ASEAN Population Coordination Unit, 69
ASEAN Population Programme, 69
Asia, 86, 88
Asian Institute of Management, 43
AWAS, *See* Angkatan Wanita Sedar.

Bani Ya'qub, 157
Berelson, 89
Berma, Madeline, 51–52, 175
Bilateral kinship system, 3
Borneo, 1
British, 5, 10–11, 17
British advisor, 6
British authorities, 6
British colonial rule, 5, 7, 55
British Empire, 125
British Military Administration, 7, 125
British North Borneo, 125
British North Borneo Company, 125
British intervention in the Malay states, 6
British resident, 6

Brunei, 126
Bugis, 5
Bukit China, 4
Bunga mas, 2
Burma, 7
Byrne, Eileen M., 71, 175

Cabinet, 21, 122
Cabinet of Ministers, 127
Capitalism, 31
Capitalist society, 4
Capital-intensive industries, 24, 26, 46
Capitalist oriented market, 10
Capitalist monetary economy, 16
Capitalistic economic development, 29
Capitalistic monetary economy, 15
Capitalists, 1
Chinese secret societies, 6
Cik Siti Wan Kembang, 2
Civil Law Act, 1956, 154
Chee, Heng Leng, 104, 175
Cheong, Siew Yoong, 29
Chia, Seow Yue, 51–52, 175
Children and Young Persons Employment Act, 1966, 144
China, 2, 6–7
Chinese, 7–8,11, 15
Chinese vernacular schools, 17
Chinese women, 12–14, 17
Cho, 89
Chong, Rosemary, 21
Christian-mission schools, 15, 17
Clarke, Andrew, 6
Coffee plantations, 14
College of Agriculture, 60
Colonial period, 1, 4–5, 10, 14–15
Colonialism, 31
Colonization, 29
Colonizers, 1, 24
Commercialization of agriculture, 31
Commercialized agriculture, 4, 10
Commonwealth, 115, 154

Commoner class, 2
Commoners, 2, 4
Constitution (Amendment) Act, 1962, 129
Consumer Association Of Penang, 146
Contraceptive, 88, 92–93, 96
Contraceptive methods used,
  Abstinence, 93
  Condom, 92
  IUD, 93
  Other female methods, 93
  Other folk methods, 93
  Pill, 93
  Rhythm, 93
  Sterilization, 75, 93
  Withdrawal, 93
Coolie trade, 13
Council of Ulamas, 9
Countries in Oceania,
  Australia, 86–87
  New Zealand, 86–87
Court officials, 2
Crown colony, 5, 125
Customary laws, 3

de Albuquerque, Alfonso, 5
Debt-bondage serfs, 2
Debt-bondage slaves, 3–4
Delayed age of marriage, 33
Department of Inland Revenue, 116
Department of Statistics, 175
Depression, 137
Developed countries in Asia,
  Hong Kong, 86–87
  Japan, 86–87
  Republic of Korea, 86–87
Dewan Muslihat, 20
Dewan Negara, *See* Legislative Assembly.
Dewan Rakyat, *See* House of Representatives.
Divide and Rule policy, 11, 17, 55
Dulang, 4, 13

INDEX 183

Dunston Ayadurai, 169, 175
Dutch, 5

Early neonatal mortality rate, 85
Emergency, 7
Emperor of China, 4
Employee's Provident Fund Ordinance, 1951, 143
Employment Act, 1955—Revised 1981, 133
English Court of Appeal, 161
Envoys, 1
Equal Rights Amendment to the American Constitution, 125
Eurasians, 8, 15
Europe, 2, 101
Europeans, 15
Executive Council, 113, 122
Expectation of life at birth by ethnic group in Peninsular Malaysia, 1957–1987, 77
Expectation of life at birth by ethnic group for females in Peninsular Malaysia, 1957–1987, 78
Expectation of life at birth for males and females among selected countries in Asia, 1986, 86
Export-oriented industrialization, 19, 24–25, 44–45
Export-oriented industries, 20, 25–26, 45

Factories and Machinery Act, 1967, 145
FAMA, *See* Federal Agricultural Marketing Authority.
Family Law, 149–150, 152
Family Planning Board, *See* Population and Family Development Board.
Faraid system, 22
Faridah Shahadan, 51–52, 175
Federal Agricultural Marketing Authority, 23

Federal Constitution, 124, 126–128, 131–133
Federal Land Development Authority, 22–23, 42, 70
Federal Legislative Council, 110
Federal Legislative Council Elections, 9
Federal Legislative Elections, 7
Federated Malay States, 6–7, 125
Federation of Malaya, 1948, 7, 18, 125–126
Federation of Women Lawyers, 138
FELDA, *See* Federal Land Development Authority.
Female labour force participation, 33, 49
Fertility trends, 75
Feudal-patriachal society, 14
Fifth Malaysia Plan, 1986–1990, 20, 22
First Malaya Plan, 1956–1960, 18, 22, 97
First Malaysia Plan, 1966–1970, 18
First World War, 137
Flexible rules of conjugal residence, 3
FMS, *See* Federated Malay States.
Fourth Malaysia Plan, 1981–1985, 20
Free Trade Zone, 25

Gambier, 13
Green Revolution, 23
Gross national product, *See* Per capita gross national product.
Guardianship of Infants Act, 1961, 153

Hamba, *See* Slaves.
Halimahton Abdul Majid, 9, 110
Hamid Arshat, 176
Hang, Li Po, Princess, 4
Heavy Industries Corporation of Malaysia, 26

Heyzer, 25
HICOM, *See* Heavy Industries Corporation of Malaysia.
Higher technology-based industries, 20, 45
House of Representatives, 127
Housewifization, 41

IBRD, *See* International Bank for Reconstruction and Development.
Ibu Zain, *See* Zain Suleiman, Hajah.
ILO, *See* International Labour Organization.
Import-substitution industrialization, 18–19
Import-substitution industries, 18, 24
Income Tax (Amendment) Act, 1975, 148
Indentured labourers, 1
Independence, 1957, 5, 7–9, 17–18, 20, 26, 41, 57, 76, 96, 107, 127
India, 2
Indian National Army, 7
Indian vernacular schools, 17
Indian women, 14, 81
Indians, 7–9, 11, 15
Indonesia, 1
Industrial Master Plan Report, 26
Industrial Relations Act, 1967, 145
Industrial Revolution, 6
Industrialization, 31–33, 41, 44, 46, 136
Infant mortality,
  neonatal, 81, 83
  post-neonatal, 81, 83
Infant mortality rate by ethnic group for Peninsular Malaysia, 1957–1987, 84
Investment Incentive Act, 1968, 25
Internationalization of production, 45
International Bank for Reconstruction and Development, 18
International Islamic University, 62
International Labour Conventions, 137, 139
International Labour Organization, 137, 139
Islam, 3
Islamic religion, 3

Jabatan Penerangan Malaysia, 122, 176
Jamilah Ariffin, 51–52, 71, 176
Janda, 158
Japanese, 7–8
Japanese Occupation, 7, 14, 17, 76, 125
Japanese invasion, 7
Jayaweera, Swarna, 72, 175
Jemaah Menteri, *See* Cabinet of Ministers.
Johor, 6, 125
Johor kingdom, 5
Jomo Kwame Sundaram, 67

Kalsom Laten, Raja Perempuan, 9
Kamal Salih, 52, 175
Kamsiah Ibrahim, 9
Kangany, See Middleman.
Kaum bangsawan, See Nobility.
Kaum Ibu, 20–21, 106–107, 109–110
Kaum Muda, 16
Kaum Tua, 16
Kaur, Amarjit, 11–12, 51–52, 177
Kaur, Manjit, 71–72, 177
Kedah, 6, 125, 156–158
Kelantan, 2, 6, 125, 157–159
KEMAS, *See* Ministry of National and Rural Development.
Kemubu, Kelantan, 23
Kerabat diraja, See Royal Family.
Kerah system, 4
Kesatuan Melayu Muda, 7
Khatijah Sidek, 109
Khek-taus, See Labour brokers.
Kitabiyah, 156

KMM, *See* Kesatuan Melayu Muda.
Krishen Jit, 122, 175

Labour brokers, 13
Labour Department, 136
Labour force, 30
Labour force participation, 12, 34
Labour force participation rates, 34, 48
Labour Force Survey, 48
Labour-intensive industries, 19, 25, 32-33, 46
Lang, Chin Ying, 51-52, 177
Law Reform (Marriage and Divorce) Act, 1976, 150, 156
Law Society of Asia, 138
Lee, Kam Hing, 122, 175
Legislative Assembly, 127
Lembaga Padi Negara, 23
LFPR, *See* Labour force participation rates.
Life expectancy, 76
Lobo, Mrs, 9
Low birth weight, 83
Light, Francis, Sir, 5
LPN, *See* Lembaga Padi Negara.

Mahathir Mohamad, 122
Major sectors of the economy,
  agriculture, 41
  business, 41
  manufacturing, 41
  services, 41
Malacca, 2, 5, 156-158
Malacca Sultanate, 2, 5
Malay College of Kuala Kangsar, 16
Malay community, 6, 10
Malay nationalist movements, 7, 106
Malay Nationalist Party, 9, 106
Malay Sultanates, 125
Malay States, 5-6
Malay women, 14, 20, 81
Malay Women Teachers Union, 8
Malays, 15

Malaya, 1, 5, 7, 10-12, 18, 125
Malayan Chinese Association, *now known as* Malaysian Chinese Association, 7, 9, 21, 107
Malayan Civil Service, *now known as the* Administrative and Diplomatic Service, 114
Malayan Communist Party, 9
Malayan Constitution, 9
Malayan Indian Congress, *now known as* Malaysian Indian Congress, 7, 9, 107
Malayan Indian Congress' Constitution, 9, 21
Malayan People's Anti-Japanese Army, 7
Malayan Union, 1946, 7, 9, 109
Malaysian Bar Council, 138
Malaysian Constitution, 110
Malaysian Medical Association, 100
Malaysian Medical Council, 100-101
Malaysian Population and Family Survey, 92-93, 105
Malaysian Trade Union Congress, 108
Malaysian women, 30-31
Male Restriction Ordinance, 1944, 14
Manderson, Lenore, 72, 122, 177
MARA, 68
Mas kahwin, 157
Masitah Mohd. Yatim, 90-91, 93, 95, 103-105, 177
Maternal and Child Health Services, 97
Maternal mortality, 76, 81, 99
Maternal mortality rate by ethnic group in Peninsular Malaysia, 1966-1986, 81
Maternity protection, 139, 141
Matrilineal society, 3
Maxwell, 29
MCA, *See* Malayan Chinese Association.

MCP, See Malayan Communist Party.
Medical Faculty, 60
Meenambal Arumugal, 21
Merchants, 1
MIC, See Malayan Indian Congress.
Middleman, 14
Migration, 1, 13–14
Ming Emperor, 2
Ministry of Agriculture, 68
Ministry of Culture, Youth and Sports, 68
Ministry of Health, 97, 99–100
Ministry of Labour and Manpower, 31, 68
Ministry of National and Rural Development, 23, 69–70
Modernization, 6, 32–33, 41
Monetary economy, 10
Mortality indicators by selected countries, 87
Mortality trends, 75
MPAJA, See Malayan People's Anti-Japanese Army.
MTUC, See Malaysian Trade Union Congress.
Muslim Law, 150, 155–156, 158–159

NACIWID, See National Advisory Council on the Integration of Women in Development.
Nahappan, Puan Sri, 9
Naisbitt, J., 174
NAP, See National Agricultural Policy.
National Advisory Council on the Integration of Women in Development, 28, 108
National Agricultural Policy, 22, 24
National Archives, 116
National Association of Women's Institute, 107
National Council for Islamic Affairs, 108
National Council of Women's Organization, 107–108

National Family Planning and Development Board, 28
National Policy for Women, 28
Nationalism, 7–8
Nationalists, 1
NAWI, See National Association of Women's Institute.
NCWO, See National Council of Women's Organization.
Negeri Sembilan, 6, 125, 156
Neo-classical economics, 30
NEP, See New Economic Policy.
New Economic Policy, 19, 21, 24–25, 33, 44
Newly Industrialized Countries, 1, 20, 45
Ng, Cecilia, 51–52, 177
NICs, See Newly Industrialized Countries.
Nik Safiah Karim, 71–72, 105, 122, 111, 177
Nobility, 2
Noor Farida Ariffin, 168, 178
Noor Laily binti Abu Bakar, 105, 178
Noraini Abdullah, 110, 113, 122, 178
Norma Mansor, 114, 117–118

O'Brien, Leslie, 54, 56, 71–72, 123, 178
Onn Jaafar, Dato, 9
Orang asli, See Aborigines.
Orang Asli Department, 98
Orang berhutang, See Debt-bondage serfs.
Other developing countries in Asia, Bangladesh, 86–87
India, 86–88
Nepal, 86–87
Pakistan, 86–88
People's Republic of China, 86–88
Sri Lanka, 86, 88
Out-migration, 10

INDEX

Pacific Rim Economy, 174
Pahang, 6, 125, 158
Palembang, 2
Pan-Malayan Malay Congress, 9
Pangkor Treaty, 1874, 6, 15
Parameswara, 2
Parliament, 110, 124
Parti Angkatan Islam, 20, 107
PAS, *See* Parti Angkatan Islam.
Patani, 2
Patriachal Malay community, 3
Patriachal society, 3, 5, 102, 132
Patriachal-caste society, 14
Patriachy, 3
Patrilineal society, 13
Pattern of female labour force participation, 33
Peasant economy, 3
Peasant women, 3–4
Peasants, 2
Penang, 5, 15, 156
Penang Free School, 15
Penghulu, 127–128, 166
Peninsular Malaysia, 1, 30, 75–81, 83–85, 90
Pensions Act, 1980, 147
Pepper, 13
Per capita gross national product, 32
Perak, 125, 158
Prenatal mortality rate, 83
Perinatal mortality rate and its components for Peninsular Malaysia, 1966–1986, 85
Perlis, 6, 125
Perniagawati, *See* Persatuan Perniagaan Wanita Bumiputra.
Persatuan Kaum Ibu, 8–9
Persatuan Perniagaan Wanita Bumiputra, 42
Philippines, 1
Pioneer Industries Ordinance, 1958, 24–25
Pondok system of religious eduction, 15

Population and Family Development Board, 92, 98
Portuguese, 5
Post-colonial period, 1, 18, 31
Post-war era, 34
Pre-colonial period, 1, 4, 31
Pre-Second World War period, 57
Prime Minister, 8
Prime Minister's Department, 28
Privatization, 19–20
Privatization of medical services and health care, 172
Production of marketable goods, 32
Public Works Department, 116
PUSPANITA, 108
Puteh Mariah, 109

Rahimah Abdul Rahman, 109
Rahman Talib Committee, 27
Raj Karim, 98, 104, 175
Raja Ijau, 2
Rajah Brooke, 125
Rakyat, See Commoners.
Razak Committee, 17
Recession, 45, 143
Reduction of fertility, 33
Rempah, 5
RISDA, *See* Rubber Smallholders Development Authority.
Royal Commission, 108
Royal Commission for Non-Muslim Marriage and Divorce, 149, 151
Royal family, 2
Rubber industry, 14
Rubber Smallholders Development Authority, 70
Ruling class, 2, 4
Rural Health Service, 97
Rural-urban migration, 25, 44

Sabah, 18, 76, 126
Sakinah Junid, 106
Salleh Omar, 165, 178
Sang Kancil Project, 69

Sarawak, 18, 76, 126
Second Malaya Plan, 1961–1965, 18
Second Malaysia Plan, 1971–1975, 19
Second World War, 6–8, 15, 17, 76, 106, 137
Selangor, 6, 125, 156
Service sector, 33, 46
Sexual harassment, 75
Sg Manik, Perak, 23
Sg Muda, Kedah, 23
Shamsiah Fakeh, 106
Shamsulbahriah Ku Ahmad, 51, 53, 178
Sharifah Hapsah Shahabudin, 101, 104–105, 178
Siam, 2, 5
Siam Protectorates, 6
Singapore, 1, 2, 7, 18, 126
Sino-Japan War, 7
Siti Noraini Jenin, 9
Siti Rohani Yahya, 50–51, 53, 178
Sixth Malaysia Plan, 1990–1995, 28
Slaves, 2
Social Security Act, 1969, 143, 145–146
SOCSO, *See* Social Security Act, 1969.
South East Asia, 2
State Assemblies, 124
State Legislative Assembly, 122
State Legislative Councils, 113, 122
Statistics Department, 30
Stillbirth rate, 85
Straits of Malacca, 5
Straits Settlements, 5–7, 15, 125
Subsistence agriculture, 3, 6, 15, 26, 31
Subsistence farming, 32
Subsistence production, 17, 31
Suffian Report, 1970, 114
Sugar plantations, 14
Sultan of Kedah, 5
Sultan of Malacca, 4
Sultan of Perak, 9

Sultan Abdullah of Perak, 6
Sultan Idris Training College, 16

Tan, Peck Leng, 67
Tan, Poo Chang, 103, 105, 77–80, 82, 84–87, 179
Tanah Melayu, 1, 2, 4
Tanjung Malim, 16
Telecoms Department, 19
Temasik, 2
Terengganu, 6, 125
Territorial chiefs, 2
Thailand, 2
Third Malaysia Development Plan, 28
Third Malaysia Plan, 1976–1980, 19, 25
Thomas, Tommy, 165, 179
Thornton, Margaret, 137, 168, 179
Tin industry, 14
Torrens Land Law, 10, 22
Torrens System, *See* Torrens Land Law.
Trusted Salary Commission of Malaya, 114
Tun Hussein Onn, 122
Tun Razak, 122
Tunku Abdul Rahman, 8–9, 122
Types of services,
    Complementary services, 46
    New services, 46
    Old services, 46

UMNO, *See* United Malays National Organization.
UMNO's Supreme Council, 20, 112
UMS, *See* Unfederated Malay States.
Unfederated Malay States, 6–7, 15
United Malays National Organization, 7, 9, 20, 107, 112
United Nations, 19, 28, 108
Universiti Hospital, 98
Universities and University College Act, 1971, 132

Universities in Malaysia,
  Universiti Kebangsaan Malaysia, 61, 63, 101
  Universiti Malaya, 57, 61, 63
  Universiti Pertanian Malaysia, 63
  Universiti Sains Malaysia, 63
  Universiti Teknologi Malaysia, 63
  Universiti Utara Malaysia, 62
Urban-industrial employment, 44
Urban industrial sector, 33
Urbanization, 32, 124
UTM, *See* Universiti Teknologi Malaysia.
Utusan Konsumer, 146
Utusan Melayu, 110
UUM, *See* Universiti Utara Malaysia.

Wanita Gerakan, 107
Wanita DAP, 107
Wanita MCA, 21
Wanita MIC, 21
Wanita UMNO, 21, 107, 112
WAO, *See* Women's Aid Organization
Warriors, 1–2

Western monopoly capitalism, 6, 10
Women Affairs Secretariat, 28, 108
Women's Aid Organization, 108
Women's Decade, 1975, 18–19, 28, 108–109
Women's Employment Bureau, 15
Women's Liberation ideology, 108, 173
Workers' Minimum Standard of Housing Act, 1966, 145
Workforce, 30, 32
Workmen's Compensation Act, 1952, 143
World Development Report, 86

Yang di-Pertuan Agong, 126, 158
Yin, Ching, 2
Young Women's Christian Association, 107
YWCA, *See* Young Women's Christian Association.

Zaharah Tamin, 9
Zain Suleiman, Hajah; *also known as* Ibu Zain, 8, 16
Zainab Baginda, 106
Zaiton Nasir, 109, 113, 123, 179